Some Good

Some Bad

Boyd E. Moffitt (signature)

Some Indifferent

Selected Poems by

Boyd E. Moffitt

A Railroad Earth Press First Edition

Copyright 1996, Boyd E. Moffitt

First Printing May 1996

All rights reserved.

No part of this book may be reproduced, stored in a retrieval system, or transmitted in any form, by any means, including mechanical, electronic, photocopying, recording, or otherwise, without prior written permission of the publisher.

Published by
Railroad Earth Press
P.O. Box 314
Canyon, California 94516-0314

Publication Data:

Boyd E. Moffitt, 1917 -
Some Good, Some Bad, Some Indifferent
Boyd E. Moffitt -- 1st ed.

ISBN 0-9652895-0-8

Printed in the United States
by the Mason Valley News, Yerington, Nevada
Thanks, Greg!
Cover Design by Luke Design Associates, Walnut Creek, California
And Thank you, Scott!

Cover photograph of Boyd E. Moffitt at 21 years of age,
July 4, 1938.

Preface

My father came to Mason Valley, Nevada nearly 45 years ago, with great regard for the land and people who populated this area. He made his home here, worked for Anaconda Copper Company, married (twice) and fathered three children. I always smile to myself when asked if I'm the eldest or youngest with respect to my two brothers, Lance and Tom. The answer would depend on who you'd ask. If you asked my mother, she'd say I was her first-born; if you asked my father, he'd have to say I was 'number two'. At any rate, all three of us have always been 'number one' with both of them, and it is that memory, along with the great fondness

I have for my father, that has made this poetry project all the more worthwhile.

Boyd Moffitt is nothing less than a 'bard' in Yerington. Many of you who have read my father's work or heard him recite his poems will undoubtedly recognize the "cowboy lariat's" voice: his fondness for the people of Mason Valley, Smith Valley and Bridgeport, California; the salty poet whose work has appeared in the Mason Valley News; and the gentle orator who has, on occasion, read from his work in venues as diverse as the local intermediate school to the Senior Citizen's Center.

My dad has written poetry that captures his feeling for the people and animals he had come to call 'friends'. And long before any of his children arrived to begin their lives in Mason Valley, our dad was penning his rhymes on sheets of notebook paper, not knowing then that his 'fourth child', a book, would also have to make its way into the hearts and hands of his audience. His great, expansive life -- from northern California, Bridgeport and Smith Valley ranch life to the high desert and copper mine of Mason Valley -- has filled his days with rich, vibrant experience. I invite you to share in the spirit of his work: enjoy his humor; reminisce with him as you read his remembrances of times past; and, if he has written about you personally, please take it lightly on the chin -- he's a salty old 'lariat', you know.

Janice Porter-Moffitt

Railroad Earth Press
Lafayette, California

Acknowledgements

In all sincerity, I wish to dedicate this book to my wife, Bea; my three children, Lance, Janice and Tom; my eight grandchildren, April, Tom Jr., Stephanie, Stacie, Larry, Linda, James and Danielle.

* * * * *

* * * * * * *

I was born in California on February 16, 1917
On a place called "Rag Hill"
The only reason I was born
They hadn't yet invented "the pill."

My schooling consisted of eight years
In a little one-room school
That's so I could be "eddicated"
And not be a complete fool.

My high schoolin' was limited
Two years of it I got
Then I went on to higher learnin'
In a college that's known as "Hard Knocks."

Table of Contents

Some Good Some Bad Some Indifferent

My Entry {By Way of Introduction}	13
My Dad	15
My Mom	17
Bows and Arrows {vs. the 25-35}	19
That Rug and Sandran	21
Camping at Chapman Creek	23
Marking Down the Loads	26
Those Primary Crusher Stairs	28
Changes Made -- Weed Heights	29
Lay-Off Time	31
Pay Day Blues	33
Sears & Roebuck	36
X-Mas Shopping at Sears	38
The Okies	40
Paying the Price	43
The Model T Ford	45
Signing Up with Anaconda, 1953	47
The Quitters	50
Happy New Year! {Written from Experience}	52
Gals of Beta Sigma Phi	55
School Days {of the 1920's}	58
Our House	60
That Old Ranch House	62
Halloween	65
Santa Comes to Our House	67
Santa Doesn't Come to Our House	68

My Rodeo Daze	69
Questions	71
Round-Up Time in Clover Valley	73
Buckskin	75
Those Phoney Deer Hunters	78
Ranchin'	81
The Little Valley Ranch	84
Our Summer Range Visit	86
Plain Tired {Written While Working (?) in a Hot Dusty Mill for Anaconda Copper}	88
My Little Old Arm Chair	91
Me and My Friends	92
Growin' Up	94
Days Gone By	97
Trapping Daze	100
Clover Valley	104
Old Nevada {1988}	107
Bridgeport Valley and the Circle H Ranch	109
Little Big or Big Enuff	112
The Big Depression {of the 1930's}	115
Smith Valley	118
Reminiscing	120
The School Fiasco	123
Young'uns "Little and Big"	125
Dr. Miller, Veterinarian	126
The Senior Center	129
VOTE	131
I'm Proud to be an American and Have the Right to Vote	133

The School Teacher's Dilemma	135
Turkey Time	137
To Whom it May Concern	139
Dr. Robin Titus, {Medicine Woman}	141
My Rustler Jeans	143
Alex Miller {A Good Friend}	145
The Church Stood Up	147
Our Mothers	149
Our Hospital	150
Mason Valley and Yerington	151
Those Darned Bankers	153
Jaywalking	155
For All Young People Everywhere	156
The People and the Valley of Bridgeport	158
Bill and Rose Kramer, Wonderful People	160
The Horse Shoein' Man	163
The Diamond B Brand and Old Joe Biglow	166
Hammonton {Near Marysville, California}	169
Clara and Lowell Hillygus	173
The Keyless Man	175

My Entry
{By Way of Introduction}

    I was born near Hammonton, California
Up there on "Rag Hill"
    And the only reason I was born
They hadn't yet invented "the pill."

    The month was February, the year '17
In the nineteen hundreds, I guess
    But then, you couldn't tell by looking
'Cause, brother, I was one hell of a mess.

    When people came and gazed at me
Oh, how they did gasp and sigh
    For they had never seen the like
Of a creature more horrible than I.

    Now, one feller said to my folks
"Now, see here, Perry and Mayme
    You'll have to sleep in separate beds
'Cause this kid here is a living shame.

    "Just look at those short bowed legs
From his hips down to his toes
    And those bat-winged ears along-side his head
And, ye Gods! What a big and crooked nose!

"And when he looks up and stares at you
With that vacant look on his pan
    You can tell he'll have a gap in his teeth
Through which you can gallop Old Dan!"

    And he will never be very tall
In fact, he will be pretty short
    So, you had better split the sheets now
Before you get another one of this sort."

    Now, I guess they took his words to heart
'Cause into different beds they did wend
    And when anyone asked them my name
They would answer, "We call him 'The End'."

    But at last I did grow to manhood
Thru' all its turbulence and strife
    And made a good, thoughtful and adoring husband
If I'm not believed, just ask my mean ol' wife.

My Dad

'Twas on the second of January
In the year of 1957
    The angels came to my father's place
And carried him off to Heaven.

He was the most gentle father
That a person ever had
    And when they took him away up there
It made me feel so mighty sad.

Now my dad was a partial cripple
All due to a broken back
    But I never knew him to complain
And I never knew him to slack.

He'd tackle any job there was
No matter if he was halt and lame
    And all the hard work he accomplished
Would put an able man to shame.

He was the most upright honest fellow
That ever drew a breath
    He was that way from the day he was born
And still that way at his death.

He never made a great name for himself
Such as Rockefeller, Astor or Ford
    But if honesty and virtue were money
He would have swept them all overboard.

He was mighty good to us children
And my mother he treated like a queen
    He very seldom said a harsh word to us
And he was never cruel or mean.

He would meet each day with a laugh and a smile
And be that way the whole day through
    Somewhere up there in the Great Beyond
God is mighty proud of the dad that we knew.

I can never remember of him spanking us
For I don't think spanking he did approve
    But when he told us to do something and meant it
We figured pretty well it was our turn to move.

When God created my father
He looked at him with a joy to behold
    He thought to himself, 'I can never do better,'
So right there and then He destroyed the mold.

Now if I could pattern my life after someone
I think nothing would be more fine
    Than to pattern my life after him
That wonderful dad of mine.

My Mom

My mother was a wonderful woman
About the best a man ever had
    A woman of strong determination
And was married many years to my dad.

    A woman, who, when her mind was set
Could do most anything she wanted
    Milk a cow, bake a cake
And never become undaunted.

    She would meet each day with a smile
On her beautiful face, so dear
    And from her lips would come a song
A song so sweet and clear.

    Songs about the olden times
When everything to her was new
    Such as "Three O'Clock in the Morning"
Or "Two Little Girls in Blue."

    She loved to go to dances
And at dancing she was great
    She'd dance and dance all evening
Until the hour was late.

    And though she danced the night away
'Til the morning began to dawn
    She'd be up doing her work
For her work, it had to go on.

She was a very determined lady
And ruled with an iron hand
   And didn't mind giving a whack
To make you understand.

   And that switch she used for whackin'
Sure had an awful sting
   My tail goes to quiverin'
When I think of that awesome thing.

   But I believe she was fair in her dealings
As I think of those days long ago
   For the pranks we played and things we did
That would make her temper glow.

   So as I end this heartfelt poem
To a wonderful mom, so dear
   I seem to hear her saying
In a voice so loud and clear,

   "Boyd! Get me a bucket of water
And a load of wood from the stack
   You better move pretty fast
Or you'll get an awful whack."

   But though she was determined and fiesty
And mighty well set in her way
   I wish that God hadn't taken her
And she was still with us here today.

Bows and Arrows
{VS. the 25 - 35}

    Now, I'm just a mediocre country guy
And I'm not expected to know too much
    About our 'politikers' and lawyer birds
And why they make certain laws and such.

    But there's one law I sure can't figure
And I don't think I can while I'm alive
    Is why they can hunt with bows and arrows
But have outlawed the 25-35.

    They say it hasn't the hitting power
(Now I sort of think this is strange)
    For I've got my deer, year after year
Out on the old cow range.

    I've buckaroo'd the woods of California
And the sagebrush of Nevada, too
    And I've rode upon a number of deer
That some bow and arrowsman slew.

    They'd been hit in a leg or a ham
Or the arrow hadn't hit hard enough
    To kill them outright right there
So why do they hand us this guff?

    Now all of the deer I've seen hide and die
Weren't wounded by a bow and arrow
    Some were there with a leg shot off
With a rifle that would shoot from here to Pt. Barrow.

So I don't think it's so much the hitting power
As it is hitting the place where you intend
    For if they aren't hit right with whatever you have
The deer will die an agonized end.

    Though we vote and elect our lawmakers
Sometimes I think it's no use to try
    For they make laws to suit themselves
And to hell with you and I.

That Rug and Sandran

    I bought my wife a woolen rug
'Twas wall-to-wall for size
    I rolled it out upon the floor
And there the darn thing lies.

    I bought it out at Reno
At a store that's known as Sears
    Now I reckon I'll get it paid for
If I live that many years.

    I really don't know the actual color
But it is sort of rosy
    It looks pretty lying there
And makes the room more cozy.

    I also bought some Sandran
(Which is a form of linoleum)
    Before I get it all paid for
I'll wish for a well of petroleum.

    Now my friend, Bud, and I we got together
And commenced laying it in the kitchen
    Before we got it measured, cut and laid
You could hear some fancy bitchin'.

    Before we got it laid down
We had to take up the old
    The folks that were living there before us
Had glued it right down cold.

Well, I hammered and sweat, swore and bitched
'Til I couldn't swear no more
    I'll tell you I was mighty put out with the man
Who had glued the linoleum to the floor.

    But at last we got it laid
And a pretty good job it was, I'll swear
    But the darn thing keeps bulging
And I have to keep whittling here and there.

    Now my wife has informed me
That the rug is crawling away from the wall
    I guess I'll get some twentypenny spikes
And nail it down with a ten-pound maul.

    So, it's just one thing after another
After you go and get wedded
    I don't see why, except for eating
That person just couldn't stay bedded.

Camping at Chapman Creek

When it's 102F. in the valley
And the land is all covered with heat
    We head for the high Sierras
To a place that's hard to beat.

'Tis the land of the mighty fir trees
And the tamaracks all growing about
    The land of the clear cold water
And the ever elusive trout.

'Tis the land of the chipmunks and squirrels
That play around the camp
    Who get into the vittles
Then up the trees do scamp.

'Tis the place of the dark red buildings
That are affectionately called the "Biffies"
    And when the seats are left up
There comes some odorous whiffies.

You wake up in the middle of the night
Having to go so mighty bad
    But to go to yonder "biffy"
Can make one awfully sad.

But usually there is a tree nearby
And at its base you can hug
    Or you may have a can within your tent
Or some old wide-mouth jug.

Some hate to get up so badly
When "Mother Nature" sounds her call
    That they lay there too darn long
And don't make it at all.

    We took Old Mick along with us
He is our little dog
    Boy, how he did saturate the trees
And every fallen log.

    And if the trees should die, Dear Lord
Upon which he has lifted his leg
    Don't be too angry with him, Dear Lord
This of You, I beg.

    It's to this land we wander
Sylvas, Moffitts and more
    To the campground along the Chapman
And to camp along its shore.

    To fish the clear cold trout streams
Of which fishing this year wasn't too good*
    Everyone except the women and Old Moffitt**
Who spent their time cooking and him getting wood.

    Some hike to Chapman Saddle
And some to Deadman's Mt. peak
    While some sit around the camp
And to each other speak.

Some talk so long and loud
That them you would like to muzzle
    Especially when you are trying to work
A brain absorbing cross-word puzzle.

They talk about most everything
But I think that you can guess
    That the words they utter most
Are just plain old B.S.

But we always have a lot of fun up there
And if everything is in the clear
    We'll all be together again
Some time this coming year.

*1980

** me

Marking Down The Loads

This marking trucks is a boring job
There isn't much to do
    Just sit around and count the loads
And watch the crusher, too.

    Of course, there are a few old lights
Mounted on a panel board
    To watch and see they don't go out
No wonder one gets bored.

    Now, my helper is of middle age
And his name is Bill
    He has been here counting loads
Since first they started the mill.

    They started the mill nearly five years ago
In October of '53
    If I sat that long and counted trucks
My sanity wouldn't be.

    A truck backs in, you mark it down
Then maybe the phone does ring
    You answer the phone and sit back down
And wonder if you marked the darned thing.

    You count all the marks on the little card
And hope your count is right
    With the counter here on the wall
Hooked up to an electric light.

But the card and the counter are seldom the same
Just like now, the counter's ahead
    Caused by a driver bumping the stop
To get mud out of the bed.

    Then you think, 'Just let it go'
For it is no disgrace
    To miss a load when marking trucks
'Cause it all goes to the same place.

    That is the reason my sanity's dimming
And I've started writing odes
    Caused from sitting here on my butt
And marking down the loads.

Those Primary Crusher Stairs

    I come to work bright and early
To start the crusher, you bet
    I feel like fighting a bob-cat
The hard hat on my head is juantily set.

    But as the day grows older
And I've climbed these long, steep stairs
    I feel more like riding a wheel chair
For I couldn't whip a hare.

    I believe these stairs are made of rubber
As from bottom to top I climb
    In fact, I know they are rubber
For they get longer every time.

    There are 166 steps from the tail of #1 belt
To the top floor where the lights are red and green
    But by the time I get there, I'll sit here and swear
There are one thousand and seventeen.

    I know these stairs are not human
As anyone can plainly see
    But what I can't see is how they know
That I'm so far from twenty-three.

    Now, these drivers think I have a pension
As I sit here on my rear
    But they wouldn't think so if they knew
What a hard time I had getting here.

Changes Made -- Weed Heights

As I sit here by the crusher
And gaze up at the town
   I often wonder if it was
A place all bare and brown.

   The flowers are all in color
The lawns are turning green
   The elm trees hold their leafy branches
Above this pretty scene.

   The iris plants are blooming
Where once a coyote strode
   The roses now are growing
On the home of an old horned toad.

   Old rattlesnakes once lay in the morning sun
Where now the gardens grow
   All made possible by the man
With water, a shovel and a hoe.

   The eagle on high gives us the eye
And also a mighty frown
   For way down below stands a man with a hoe
In what was once a prairie dog town.

   The rabbits once lunched on plain sagebrush
And carried their own canteens
   But now today, you can hear them say,
"I'll have some more of those string beans."

This has all taken place since 1952
When man first planted the sod
   All made possible by the man and his hoe
And the Almighty Hand of God.

Lay-Off Time

    If Anaconda should close its gates
Come some wintery morning
    Oh, what a sad place it would be
For most everyone would be in mourning.

    They wouldn't know which way to turn
Nor just which way they'd go
    They'd be like a chicken with its head cut off
Ah, they'd be feeling mighty low.

    Most would stand and stare into space
Not seeing a darned thing funny
    But I would sit in my old easy chair
And draw my rocking chair money.

    They tell me I can draw sixty a week
For not doing a blessed tap
    To pass up a deal like that
I'd sure be an awful sap.

    And if my creditors became put out
For me not paying my bills
    They'd just have to wait for work to start again
Up here in these old copper hills.

    Now maybe this would be a good lesson
For everyone who is concerned
    Maybe the stores won't give so much credit
And a man won't spend more than he's earned.

But it seems that some will never learn
The true value of a dollar
   'Cause when things get tough and they haven't one
All they want to do is holler.

   They spend their dough like a drunken sailor
Buy anything and everything that comes along
   Should they have something left over
That goes for wine, women and song.

   Yes, people are mighty strange creatures
They will rant and rave and cuss this place
   But the minute they hear it might shut down
A scared and vacant look appears on their face.

   Now, many people say they need the work
(And I'm not doubtin' but what it's true)
   To buy their families some clothing
And some meat to put in a stew.

   But with me it's a little different
I don't know, maybe I'm just funny
   For I don't really need the work
But boy! I sure do need the money.

Pay Day Blues

Oh, I went to the window down at the office
To draw my two weeks' pay
    The rain was coming down pretty good
On that 22nd of May.

I grabbed my check in a hurry
And towards my car I did fly
    Almost got run over
By a car that was passing by.

But finally I got to my car
And gave it a great big crank
    Pointed its nose toward town
And to the First National Bank.*

There I shelled out some dough
On my loan and on my truck
    Then I thought to myself
I'm sure a fast guy with a buck.

I made my payments and banked the rest
Just like a man with a pile of dough
    But anyone who thought so, would sure be surprised
If they saw me making payments on bills that I owe.

After the bank there is the grocery
Where goes some more of my swag
    I pay 30 bucks for one week's vittles
And carry it out in one paper bag.

After the grocer there is the hardware
And maybe the drugstore, too
    Where at each I have a charge account
And there's most always a balance due.

    At last I get back home
And brother I sure hate to look
    At all the bills I've made payments on
And the balance in my old check book.

    I sits down and figures the balance
There's a little left over, it appears
    But God! I just happened to remember
I didn't send the payment to Sears!

    Well, I writes them out a payment
And sealed it good and tight
    Took it to the post office
So it would be in the mail that night.

    I walks into the Post Office
And there I stood in a trance
    For lying there in my mail box
Was a bill for my son's insurance.

    As long as I was there I paid that, too
Then out the door I did scoot
    I felt like a feller that's all dried out
And long overdo for a toot.

    I ambles back home to my family
And hope the balance in my checkbook I didn't botch
    For by my figures we could get by for two weeks
If our belts we took up another notch.

    Seriously, we are darned lucky
And here we have it darned nice
    For if the Japanese had won the war
We would be on a diet of rice.

    So though we might feel disgruntled
And at times must rob Peter to pay Paul
    It sure is nice to be able to pay on our bills
Than to have no money at all.

* Now First Interstate Bank

Sears & Roebuck

    Good old Sears and Roebuck
With their easy payment plan
    It's the best thing since the wheel
To benefit the working man.

    Once you have your credit established
You can order to your hearts' content
    The down payment is very small
In fact, you need not pay a cent.

    You can order all sorts of items
From tires to hoseries
    Yes sir, most everything you can think of
Excepting groceries.

    And if sometime in the future
They should handle that line
    The people would be overjoyed
And Sears business would be mighty fine.

    For years and years they have sent out catalogs
Whose pages were wide and thick
    And they used to serve a double purpose
'Til the pages became so dog-gone slick.

    Those were the days before fancy plumbing
And those little houses sitting out alone
    Never did seem entirely complete
Without a catalog by the throne.

You could rest and make your wishes
From this wishbook's many pages
    For there was most anything in it
That was of interest to all the ages.

    Then you would look for something special
It would make you so mad you could shout
    To turn to that section
And find the page had been torn out.

    Now these days with the fancy plumbing
Just don't seem homelike at all
    For instead of an old Sears catalog
It's a roll of tissue on the wall.

    So now after we get our new issue
No longer through the old one we browse
    For it can serve no double purpose
Since running water came to our house.

    Now they are thinning out Sears
And the catalogs will be no more
    I guess we'll have to patronize
The K-Mart and Wal-Mart stores.

X-mas Shopping at Sears

I told my wife to jot things down
That she would like from old St. Nick
And I would send a letter off to him
After I had made my pick.

She started to write things down
My God! How that list did mount
I looked at my checkbook and I thought,
"You've had it, bank account."

First she wanted some silverware
Then she wanted a purse
Then she wanted a food-grinder
I'll tell you it got worse and worse.

I can't begin to tell you
All the things she wanted on that list
But I can really tell you
She didn't want to be missed.

Now this was just her personal list
Of what she wanted Santa to bring
Then there are those three kids of ours
Who had their song to sing.

Of course they wanted everything
They saw in the old wish book
By the time they had their lists made out
It sure had old pa upon the hook.

    I took their lists and went to town
Out here about 80 miles
    And all the way on that trip
There wasn't any smiles.

    But by the time I got to Sears
I felt better by quite a bit
    And went on such a shopping spree
I figured I must be half lit.

    But I know I had nothing to drink
Of anything with alcohol
    In fact, I was in such a dither
I had nothing to drink at all.

    My bill at Sears was almost paid
Just a couple of payments more
    But, by-gollies, I was another year in debt
Before I left that store.

    It's nice to have that charge account
When you X-mas shop at Sears
    But why in the heck can't X-mas come
Just once in every ten years.

    Yes, it's nice to have that charge account
When the wife and kids make out their list
    And buy for them at X-mas time
And hope you, yourself, don't get missed.

The Okies

The Okies came to California
Nearly thirty years ago
    Grabbed the jobs from the native sons
By working for wages terribly low.

They had nothing of any value
I'll tell you, they were beat
    Their clothes were in tatters
And they had very little to eat.

I've seen them camped out in a tent
(If they were lucky enough to have the same)
    Or a shelter made of cardboard
It surely was a shame.

Yes, I've seen them camp in winter
Out there on the cold damp earth
    Men, women and children
And some women giving birth.

As I said, their clothes were ragged
Many had no shoes upon their feet
    And the only pants they had
Were patches on patches on the seat.

Once I said to a little girl
As she was passing me by,
    "In winter, with no shoes or socks,
It looks like you would die."

She looked at me and I could see
That she was mighty close to tears
    Then she gazed at her feet and said to me,
"I haven't worn shoes for years."

I guess she was telling the truth
For bare feet seemed to bother her none at all
    'Cause I never spied shoes upon her feet
Be it Summer, Winter, Spring or Fall.

Now 'twas down around that fruit country
That my dad owned a little store
    And you could see these things taking place
As you stood in his back door.

But my dad was too kind-hearted
To have a business of this kind
    For the food he dished out gratis
Soon put him way behind.

And when he sold this business
To a man by the name of Brooks
    He had hundreds and hundreds of dollars
Chalked up in his credit books.

Now, I felt very sorry for these Okies
'Cause they had it mighty bad.
    But after looking at his books
I felt more sorry for my dad.

Some of the people once had good homes
Back there from where they came
   But the dust covered over their property
So they really weren't to blame.

   Of course they nudged the Californians aside
While a niche for themselves they were carving
   But show me a man who won't do that
If he and his family are starving.

   You may wonder why they didn't go on welfare
Now let me make this perfectly clear
   There wasn't any welfare
On which you could set your rear.

   You had to make it by yourself
If you wanted to get ahead
   If you couldn't make it by yourself
Then let me tell you, you were dead.

   It matters not from where you hail
This is the way I feel
   A man is a man from any state
Or he is just a heel.

Paying the Price

I came to this place in '53
And didn't owe a cent
    Now today, I can sit and say,
"I'm not broke but I'm badly bent."

    I had a few hundred in the checking
About the same in the savings, too
    But I thought I had to have new things
Boy, how my surplus flew.

    I thought if I came here and settled
A fortune could be made
    But somewhere in the shuffle
My fortune became mislaid.

    But maybe some day in the future
I'll do myself a good deed
    Not buy everything I want
But just the things that I need.

    But I guess I'm not so bad off
In fact, it could be a lot worse
    For I could be so far in debt
My only relief would be a black hearse.

    Though I may be downhearted
And down in the dumps I may get
    All I have to do is remember
I'm not the only one in debt.

    I don't blame the company
For the wages have been fair
    I have no one to blame
For my deep and dark despair.

    Now take the advice of an old fool
No matter where you roam
    If you haven't the money to pay the bill
You had better stay at home.

The Model T Ford

    I can remember back to days gone by
When I was just a lad
    To the days of the Model T Ford
And the effects it had on my dad.

    He was used to a team of horses
And drove them wherever he did go
    So consequently when he bought his Ford
It wouldn't stop when he hollered, "Whoa!"

    He used to park beside the house
That stood upon a hill
    If the house hadn't been there
He would have been a' going still.

    I'll bet if you could find that Ford
Which he bought around 1920
    You would have no trouble telling it was his
For the dents in the fenders were a' plenty.

    He would try to start it on a cold morning
And crank so hard I thought over he would keel
    Then as a last and only resort
He would jack-up one back wheel.

    Then if the "Tin Lizzy" wouldn't start
After using all the various courses
    He would amble out to the barn
And hitch up his team of horses.

That old Model T was sure independent
It cared not for ramming a house or a barn
    It cared not where it stopped or stalled
And it cared not, when cranked, about breaking an arm.

    And when we went for a ride on Sunday
My dad had always had a cud of chewing
    To duck and dodge the curves he spit
Sure did take some doing.

    When that Ford was running right
I'm right here to tell you, man
    On a hill the motor chugged away
And kept saying, "I think I can, I think I can."

    And when you came to a long steep downhill
It mattered not if you had brakes
    You just cut a fair-sized tree
And tied it in its wake.

    You could be driving it along the road
Just sitting up there as big as life
    When all of a sudden a front tire would blow
And then the thing would jackknife.

    There's many a thing could happen
As you went for a ride in that Ford
    But the uppermost thing in everyone's mind
It wouldn't send you to meet your Lord.

Signing Up With Anaconda, 1953

    I came to work here seven years ago
Or it will be the 21st of September
    Wandered into the personnel office
And said I'd like to be a member.

    Told them I would like a job
In either the mine or the mill
    'Cause the grass was pretty dry
On yonder side of the hill.

    Now, Joe looked at me in a peculiar way
And I sure knew the reason why
    I figured right there and then I'd get no job
Because I have one bad eye.

    He said he didn't think there was a chance
But as long as I had come so far,
    "Go on down and see the doc,
But you may have to pull him out of a bar."

    I went on down to see the doc
And waited an hour and a half in line
    For him to examine some others
And then for him to get to mine.

    He looked me over pretty darned good
Then he shook his head right hard
    I expected him to tell me right then and there
I was ready for some old bone yard.

He said I wasn't in too bad of shape
Except for my bum left eye
    But he was afraid I couldn't pass
And there was no use to try.

    But then I began to chat with him
And we talked there back and forth
    He became pretty well interested
When I said I knew of his folks up north.

    Finally at last I won him over
After giving him a big song and dance
    He gave me a note to the personnel
And said maybe they would take a chance.

    I came on back to the personnel
And I gave that note to Joe
    He said he had to see a man
As back through the office he did go.

    In about five minutes he came on back
And said that they would give me a trial
    I signed affidavits and some other papers
Of them there was quite a pile.

    I was on probation for three whole months
I felt like a feller who had sinned
    Who had been arrested for some hold-up
And a sentence on me had been pinned.

I also filled out my application
Listing all my jobs in years gone by
    Told them where and when I was born
And also told them the reason why.

At length I got all signed up
Then they sent me back to see a man
    He said, "You sure have had a lot of jobs,"
As over my application he did scan.

I told him that was sure the truth
That I had held many a station
    And that I had thought of a dozen more
Since I had filled out my application.

So here I've been for seven years
Doing jobs too numerous to mention
    And barring death or job lay-off
I'll be here 'til I get my pension.

All in all it's a good place to work
And though I didn't think I'd stay for awhile
    I look back over these seven years
And thank the company for that trial.

25 Years Later -- 1978

Yes, I'm glad they gave me a chance
And I stayed 'til I got my pension
    Now I can sit back in my easy chair
And only from my wife get any dissention.

The Quitters

    They leave old Anaconda
To go elsewhere to make their pile
      But then you will see them returning
In just a little while.

    They tell you the grass is greener
On yonder side of the fence
      So why do they ever return?
It certainly doesn't make any sense.

    Yes, I've seen them leave this job
To go where the dough came thick and fast
      But they return with heads hanging low
And say that the job didn't last.

    If their conscience is bothering them
As to why they acquired no wealth
      They'll tell you in a very sickly way
That they returned on account of their health.

    I guess at that they aren't lying
For when you don't eat as much as you should
      Your old belly gets pretty darned lank
So a person can't feel very good.

    When they go to leave here
They forget this mighty low rent
      They don't take time to consider
That in other places for it, your check is half spent.

Oh, I can't deny the fact that I
Sometimes, too, get itchy feet
   But where could I go in these times so slow
And have a nice comfortable seat?

   Yes, there are times I'd like to leave
And my job here I'd like to shirk
   But then I get to thinking
That in some other job I might have to work.

   So I guess that I will stay here
And help to put out the concentrate
   Then sit and draw my Social Security
Upon that retirement date. (65 years)

Happy New Year!
{Written from Experience}

'Twas New Year's Eve in the valley
The revelers were whooping it up downtown
   There were parties and dancing, liquor galore
And everyone playing the clown.

   Oh, what fun these people had
At winning, dining and dancing
   But as the night drew near to dawn
They had slowed way down on their prancing.

   They wandered home about five in the morn
Perhaps the husband was driving
   The wife lay slumped down in the seat
And never knew at home were arriving.

   Or maybe the husband lay slumped in the seat
With his wife clutching the wheel
   And when they arrived at their home
Into the house they would reel.

   The noise-makers and hats were scattered about
Grim reminders of last night's thirst
   It never once entered their sodden heads
That their kids would be up first.

   Old pa and ma lay snoring in the sack
Nothing but sleep on their minds
   When an ungodly noise made them leap out of bed
As though firecrackers were tied to their behinds.

It was just little Tommy who had gotten out of bed
That fateful New Year's morn
    And had decked himself out in a cute little hat
And had found a dad-blasted horn.

    Now, ma and pa had throbbing domes
In fact, they were one awful sight
    And the noise of that horn this early morn
Didn't sound as good as it did last night.

    Poor Tommy would have got a thumping
Had he stayed there and stood his ground
    But all that saved him and his skin
Was his folks' heads going 'round and 'round.

    Now, ma put on her old housecoat
And fixed the coffee to brew
    Dug out a can of tomato juice
And a bottle of aspirin, too.

    Pa laid back upon the sack
Just togged-out in his X-mas shorts
    And thought to himself, "Why, oh why,
Did I take so many snorts?"

    They sat and drank their coffee and juice
And swallowed the aspirins
    Gazed at each other out of blood-shot eyes
With vacant and foolish grins.

They vowed they would never do it again
(But this is too hard to believe)
For I'm telling you and I'll bet that it's true
They'll be right back there next New Year's Eve.

Gals of Beta Sigma Phi

They are going out on the town next Friday night
Those gals of Beta Sigma Phi
    To get their bellies full of vittles
Wine and just plain old "red-eye".

They'll be down there making whoopee
'Till the wee hours of the night
    While the poor old men are watching the kids
And trying to keep them out of a fight.

Then there are those who are on 'swing'
Who trudge to work feeling a little bitter
    And when he gets home at midnight
Digs down deep to pay the sitter.

I don't know how many will be at the blow out,
I imagine most all the members will be there
    Along with some of those Greeks they talk about
Such as Socrates, Hippocrates, Homer and Menander.

They'll have great fun while their money holds out
Then homeward they will reel
    And never a thought enters their sodden heads
Of the next day and how they will feel.

They'll park the car in about the middle of the street
Somewhere in the vicinity of their house
    Creep out and in through the door
Trying to be as quiet as a little old mouse.

But they forget about the coffee table
That sits there in the room
    And when their shin and it come together
It sounds like a sonic boom.

    At last she gets to the bedroom
After the bathroom where she's been
    Sits down on the edge of the bed
And gently massages her shin.

    She lies down on her side of the bed
Just trying to be so still
    While her old man on the other side
Is laughing fit to kill.

    Oh, she looked so nice the night before
Just like a queen in all her glory
    But next morning at the breakfast table
Was quite a different story.

    Her hair stuck out in all directions
Just like a "porkies" quills
    And to look into those blood-shot orbs
Gives you ice-cold chills.

    And you ask her how the party was
And what was that awful din
    She looks at you with murder in her eyes
As she reaches down and rubs her shin.

    Oh, they have great fun at these Greek parties
And for them to go I'm glad they are able
    But boys, for God's sake don't laugh
When she bangs into the coffee table.

p.s.

    I only kid about their drinking
I don't believe they take a taste
    I don't know if they don't like it
Or they're afraid it will add inches to their waist.

School Days
{of the 1920's}

When I was a young'un growing up
(At that I didn't grow up too far)
We went on horseback to a one-room school
We didn't go there in a car.

Yes, we rode our horses to school
No matter if it was a sunny or rainy day
Just left them tied up at the fence
And partaking of post hay.

Now, the lunches we carried to school
Weren't on the better side
'Cause by the time noon came around
The sandwiches all had dried.

And if we forget and left them
Out there in the old school lot
Just like the kids have them today
We sure did have them hot.

Those old bacon or bean sandwiches
Which seemed our daily fare
Sure tasted good at noon
Even though left out in the hot air.

The teacher had a lot of time with each kid
(I can remember as well now as then)
In that little one-room schoolhouse
Was the total sum of ten.

We didn't get into too much trouble
There wasn't much misbehaving
   Except for the two eighth graders
Who were darned near grown and shaving.

But at that they weren't too bad
If they were, they were dead
   For their dads would take a latigo strap
And their butts would be a cherry red.

The nearest town was 10 miles away
Out across those rolling plains
   And the ground would mire a saddle blanket
When came the winter rains.

We couldn't go to a convenience store
And eat things made of sugar and honey
   It wasn't because we wouldn't like to have
But we wouldn't have had the money.

Now as I look back on it all
There is just one thing that brings me pain
   We couldn't ride our horses to town at noon
And there upon "drag" Main.

p.s.
   These were the days when the teacher's word was law
And you didn't see kids running loose
   They didn't run to the police when popped on the butt
And holler, "Child Abuse!"

Our House

Some keep their houses like pig pens
While some are spotlessly clean
　I guess we keep our house
Somewhere in between.

　My hats are thrown on the table
Although we have a hat rack in the hall
　My wife has papers strewn about
And my shoes are lined up by the living room wall.

　The floors are vacuumed every once in awhile
(That is a must)
　Then maybe if we feel like it
We'll throw a rag at the dust.

　Some cobwebs may hang here and there
And when the sun hits them just right
　I can't bear to knock them down
For their laciness is a pretty sight.

　I guess the windows do need washing
But they are so dog-gone tall
　I can't climb that high on a ladder
For fear that I might fall.

　Now, if I forget to wipe my shoes
There may be dirt or mud on the floor
　But why get excited
That's what I bought the vacuum for.

So how we keep our house
Isn't a mortal sin
It's home sweet home to us
And the kind we like to live in.

That Old Ranch House

    I well remember the old ranch house
That stood there on the W.K.
    It was built for a pretty big family
Which was normal for that golden day.

    There was one bedroom on the bottom
And three on the upper deck
    When things became icy
We'd triple up, by heck.

    The big rock fireplace in the living room
Threw out a lot of heat
    For a fire made from yellow pine wood
Was mighty hard to beat.

    But after the fire went out
And the heat no longer came up the stairs
    It got pretty darned cold
Even with lots of covers and "Long John" underwear.

    The dining room was connected to the kitchen
And we spent most of our idle time in there
    Playing cards and other games
While someone braided a rope made of hair.

    Then there might be a leppy calf or bummer lamb
That we brought in from the icy chills
    We took darned good care of them
For they helped to pay the bills.

The old wood range over by the wall
Used to fire my wrath
    When I stooped over too far
While taking my Saturday night bath.

It may have been a Home Comfort
Or a Wedgewood, they both were pips
    But when you stooped too far
You were branded across both hips.

It was the meeting place for all
No matter the time of day
    It made no difference who or what you were
You had to eat before you went on your way.

But if you rode up with intentions to eat
And left your horse tied up outside
    You better not let the boss catch you
Or he sure as hell would have your hide.

First you take care of your horse
Before you sit down to eat
    If he isn't taken care of
You may go out the door but not on your feet.

Now, I guess that's about all for the house
Except one mighty important thing
    It's that little house out in the back
And the relief to you it might bring.

It was built on yon side of the woodpile
So that women, when they had to "go"
    Could bring back an armload of wood
For the woodbox, which was usually low.

Now sometimes I miss all this
Where everything was cozy and nice
    Yes, I even miss that little house
Where in the winter the seat was like ice.

Halloween

They come up to the door
Dressed in costumes nice and neat
   Knock on the door or ring the bell
And holler, "Trick or Treat!"

   You give each one some candy
As they hold out their little hand
   And you wish you could give more
To the smallest in the band.

   But you try to give each one the same
So that tricks they do not play
   And then I started remembering back
To how things were in my younger day.

   Those were the days of the old back house
We'd wait for some man to get seated before
      We'd run up behind it
And push it over onto its door.

   Then if he hollered and cussed too much
And really carried on
   If his family didn't get him out
We'd leave him there 'til dawn.

   Or we would take a rancher's horse buggy
(And this sure isn't any yarn)
   We'd take it all apart
And put it together again on top of the barn.

Yes, we were ornery little buggers
But it sure made our mouths go slack
    When the rancher saw us do it
And then made us put it back.

    So as I look back on things we did
Especially on Halloween
    It's nice to have a lot of fun
But don't do as we did -- keep it clean.

Santa Comes to Our House

    Santa is coming thru' the sky
I can hear the sleigh bells ringing
    I can hear old Blitzen snorting
And I can hear the carolers singing.

    I hear him stop upon the roof
And say to himself, "By Jiminy,
    How do these people get along
With such a little chimney?"

    But I guess he had the powers
To make himself as thin as a rail
    For he didn't seem to have any trouble
As down the chimney he did sail.

    He placed the presents under the tree
Ate the cookies and drank the milk placed there
    Shot up the chimney, got in his sleigh
And vanished off into the air.

    Next morning as I gazed at the presents
I wished him a lot of ill-will
    For there hung on the tree, where he put it,
Was a blamed old MasterCard bill.

Santa Doesn't Come to Our House

    I hear old St. Nick coming back
I wish that old guy would stay away
    It seems he was here last
Just the other day.

    I hear the same old sleigh bells ringing
I can hear Blitzen snorting again
    And the carolers singing the same old songs
It brings me a lot of pain.

    But I can't hear him this year upon the roof
Complaining of the chimney that is small
    In fact, he just went on by
And didn't stop at all.

    He did drop a note down the chimney
As he sailed right on by
    Stating nothing was coming my way
So there was no use to cry.

    It said the reason he wasn't stopping
Wasn't because I had wished him ill-will
    It was because I hadn't paid
My last year's MasterCard bill.

My Rodeo Daze

    I started out making the shows
Several years ago
    Figured I could make some dough
In some old rodeo.

    I started in at ropin'
It seemed the simplest thing
    I caught my calf and dogged him
But I had forgotten my piggin' string.

    So of course the judge waved his flag
I knew that it meant "no time"
    And when that show had ended
I hadn't made a dime.

    I then tried the saddle broncs
I'll tell you boys, they were rough
    And after my falls didn't get any easier
I knew it was too damned tough.

    They told me that to win any money
An eleven second ride was a must
    But I didn't win any money in that
Cause I watched the last few seconds from the dust.

    I then tried my hand at bull-dogging
But I was such a little cuss,
    The steer would take me right along with him
And not raise any fuss.

    But one time I did get one down
(I guess he must have fell)
    But he quickly threw me off
And left like a bat out of hell.

    So I soon quit the rodeos
God, how my folks did laugh
    When I went back to my gentle cow horse
And roping the milk cow's calf.

    But let them laugh as they want to
For that rough stock brought too much pain
    And I'll leave it to those who like it
And never go rodeoin' again.

Questions

I've wondered around these old mining camps
Which flourished a hundred years or so ago
    And wondered if they were wild and woolly
Or were they awfully dull and slow?

    And cast off things lying about
What stories could they tell
    Were they happy in what they did
Or was theirs a living hell?

    That old frying pan lying there
With its bottom all rusted through
    Did it fry eggs for some rich 'nabob'
Or some poor guy with kids quite a few?

    And that old wood stove down in the draw
With its oven and door bashed in
    Did it languish in some rich home
Or did it cook meals for a bunch of men?

    That old bedstead out in the sage
How did it meet its doom?
    Was it a workbench for an older couple
Or a playpen for a younger bride and groom?

    And that old ore wagon down beside the mill
(With the wheels removed by some thief)
    Was yours a heavily-laden load
Or were you just used in relief?

And those old horse shoes in the blacksmith shop
How did you earn your keep?
    Were you trod upon by a one-ton horse
Upon these hills so steep?

    Yes, I'd like to hear them tell some tales
About these mines from which ore was wrested
    In those days of old when men were bold
And women were doubly double-breasted.

Round-Up Time in Clover Valley

    Oh, I'd like to be in Clover Valley
When they round-up in the fall
    I'd like to see the horses running
And listen to the cattle bawl.

    I'd like to hear the creek of my saddle
As I get astride in the early morn
    And as my cayuse goes to buckin'
To reach wildly for the horn.

    Just to hear the bit-chains tinkling
As he swings his head to and fro
    Just to hear my bat-wings swishing
As out through the timber I go.

    Just to hear an old cow bawling
With never a stop nor a lull
    Wondering if she's lost her calf
Or if she is looking for a bull.

    I will help her if she's lost her calf
For no doubt he's out there all alone
    But should it be a bull she's looking for
Well, then she is strictly on her own.

    Just to watch my dog as he trots along
And of you, Dear Lord, I beg
    Don't let all the pine trees die
Upon which he has lifted his leg.

    Just to hear my spurs a jinglin'
As they are bound there on my feet
    I'll tell you boys, I'd be in heaven
'Cause, for me, this life can't be beat.

    All this I had a few years ago
When I was a single buck
    But now that I'm hitched and have some kids
I reckon with Anaconda I'm stuck.

    But this job may not last forever
This job in this hot dusty mill
    And if it should end before I do
I'll head right back over the hill.

    Back there to those evergreen mountains
Back to where the waters run down from the snow
    Unroll my "turkey" in the old bunk house
And from that range no more will go.

    For that is sure the life, boys
For a feller such as I
    To be out with the horses and cattle
Out where the mountains seem to meet the sky.

Buckskin

I came up here to the Buckskin mine
A watchman for to be
    Just a sittin' here in the trailer
And a scannin' the road for to see.

    To see if there's anyone a comin'
Up that old rough and rocky road
    But I hardly see anything a stirrin'
Except maybe an unpassionate or a horny toad.

    I gaze across this desert valley
And see some grazing cattle
    To get enough to fill their guts
Seems to be one hell of a battle.

    And as I gaze on the ranch below
And it, too, is known as Buckskin
    I'm a wonderin' why they don't feed them
'Cause these critters are a gettin' mighty thin.

    But actually they ain't so bad
In this country without any trees
    And I'm a wonderin' how one would look
Stuffed down in my old deep freeze.

    'Bout the time I got him in the freezer
At the place where I'm a boardin'
    Some officer would say to me,
"Come and shake hands with the warden."

And as I'm a sittin' behind the bars
Feelin' mighty down-cast and bitter
    Some geezer will be a' sleepin' with my wife
And partakin' of that damned old critter. (The cow, too!)

    But then there is some other life
Like now I see a chipmunk a' skitterin' by
    With one eye cocked up yonder
At that red-tailed hawk up in the sky.

    And at times I see some wild horses
On the ridges or the valley below
    And I watch the old stud, who is the boss,
Make the mares go where he wants to go.

    And I hear the hungry coyotes
As they sing from some hill-top,
    So I feed them the scraps from supper
And any other slop.

    Then there are some other animals
Who stay out there alone
    They must be of the Jewish faith
For they won't bother with any ham bone.

    Now the blackbirds and the pigeons
Live in mine shafts on the hill
    And every evening go to Compston's feed lot
Their poor old bellies to fill.

And when they come back from feedin'
(Sure, they are good and kind old ma's)
   For they have something for their kids
Crammed down in their little old craws.

Yes, it's pretty nice up here
Where I can gaze all around
   For this ex-cowboy and miner
Wasn't meant for any town.

Those Phoney Deer Hunters

    Gather in your cattle and horses
Lest it bring you a lot of sorrow
    Lock them in a high, tight corral
For deer season opens tomorrow.

    Stand ye there as a sentinel
A 105 cannon by your side
    For there are those who know no difference
'Twixt a beef and venison hide.

    Now maybe they do know the difference
But just don't seem to care,
    Figure it should be good eating
'Cause it's all covered with hair.

    These are the guys who have no business
With any kind of a gun
    They'll shoot at anything that moves
In the brush or out in the sun.

    They'll gather around the fire at night
Telling tales of what huntsmen they be
    Trying their best to out-lie each other
Egged on with a jug of whiskey.

    They'll drink and lie 'til the wee hours
Then into their sacks they'll fall
    They aren't up here to go deer hunting
They are only here to have a ball.

Well, perhaps it is a ball they're having
For it's every person to his taste
    But it isn't fair to the real hunter
As they cause him his money to waste.

    These phonies holler and sing and make merry
'Til the darkness turns into dawn
    Then when the hunters go out in the morning
The deer have all long gone.

    Gone from the noise and confusion
That erupted so loudly last night
    Gone from that hated man-smell
Gone far o'er the mountains in their flight.

    Gone from the guns that are booming
From canyon to mountain top
    Running for self-preservation
Run 'til they are ready to drop.

    So the phonies return from their hunting
Without an ounce of meat
    But under an old cedar tree
They spy a heifer so neat.

    Up comes a high-powered rifle
And a hole in her side does appear
    They think to themselves this is much better
Than any kind of a deer.

So lock up your livestock, ranchers
For tomorrow deer season does start
   Lock them up and stand guard
Or you and your livestock may part.

Ranchin'

I guess I could be away from ranch life
For fifty years or sich
　But when the spring begins to greenin'
My feet begin to itch.

　Itchin' for that old homestead
Where I grew up to be a man
　And I thinks to myself I'll go back there
As soon as I possibly can.

　Just to see the manure dust risin'
As the horses race 'round the corral
　Just to step in that big old barn
And whiff that ammoniated smell.

　Just to ride out in the pasture
Where the cows are slick and fat
　Decked out in a pair of Justins
And a twenty-gallon hat.

　Just to wake up early in the morning
When the dawn begins a new day
　Just to lie there for awhile
And smell the new-mown hay.

　Just to hitch up a couple of hay-burners
To a wagon or a rake
　And go out in the hayfields
And there some hay do make.

Now, I've listed some of the brighter things
That cause my feet to itch
    But then there is the darker side
That just causes me to bitch.

    First, there are those old post holes
Where the rocks grow big and tight
    And every inch you gain
Costs one hell of a fight.

    And the wires you tack upon the posts
Aren't on the smoothest side
    And when one slips and grabs you
You lose about a mile of hide.

    And the hay you joyously put up in summer
Is just lying there in the stack
    Waiting to be fed to the old cow brutes
To take up their hungry slack.

    Just waiting to be loaded in the wagon
No matter if it's rain or snow
    'Cause those old cows must be fed
No matter if it's forty below.

    And the barn with the ammoniated odor
That at first I was talking about
    Well, sometime in the early spring
You have to clean it out.

So, first you hitch up a team of horses
To a spreader or a wagon
　　Then you start in and pitch manure
'Til you run to the door a' gaggin'.

　　Now, as I sit in my easy chair
In the bowels of the earth below
　　I get to thinking of the darker side
And my feet don't itch me so.

　　Besides, I've been here such a long time
That to go back to work would be a sin
　　So I'll just relax in my old arm chair
And as a rancher, I'll be a has-been.

The Little Valley Ranch

As I sit here alone tonight
My mind is never free
    Of thoughts of that Little Valley Ranch
And what it meant to me.

    It was there, along in the thirties,
Where Clover, Lil and I
    Would ride our old cow ponies
To where the mountains meet the sky.

    Now, they were daughters of the owner
While I was just a hand
    Though you wouldn't know by looking
But what I was one of the clan.

    I resembled Old Ned, they tell me,
From my head clear down to my toes
    Short, bowlegged and stocky
And that ever prominent nose.

    Old Ned was born in Switzerland
Along about 1883
    Came to this country as a boy
To this good old land of the free.

    He was a man of distinction
His name was one of renown
    If a neighbor needed a helping hand
There Old Ned could be found.

We were all so happy together
There on the old NB
   Until a greetings I got
Then it was the army for me.

   After three long years I returned there
Thinking it would be the same
   But I sure was fiddle-footed
And I took off again.

   For several years I wondered around
Working at this or that
   Be it a service station or a store
Or skinning a D4 "Cat".

   I've traveled over the country
But nothing I ever did see
   Could compare with Little Valley
Back there at the old NB.

   Now, as I sit here in this old arm chair
My mind, how it doth stray
   To that ranch back in the mountains
Where I would love to return someday.

Our Summer Range Visit

We traveled out through the mountains
To where they seemed to meet the sky
   To the green of Clover Valley
Just my Little Pard and I.

   Near the head of the Susan River
Where the waters run cold and clear
   Where the fish swim in the shadows
And right close by, the deer.

   Where the cattle graze on the meadows
Where the grass grows lush and green
   Where the chipmunks play in the tamaracks
'Tis a sight you never before have seen.

   Where the people all are so friendly
As they go on day after day
   Working with their cattle and horses
Or when they take time to play.

   Now, my "Little Pard" is a five-year-old
And, in fact, he is quite a lad
   He sure enjoyed every moment of it
But then, so did his dad.

   He was riding a gentle Buckskin
Whose name was Buck, of course
   You would thought him King of the Cowboys
Upon that good old horse.

He was riding him around through the yard
A place where he shouldn't have been (my fault)
   When a guy rope holding the water tank
Caught him under the chin.

   Now, I was taking some pictures
And wasn't paying him no mind
   But I turned around and saw him sail
Right over Old Buck's behind.

   Well, I rushed right over and picked him up
For he had landed with quite a force
   When asked if he was hurt or not
He said, "No, but where is the G.D. horse!"

   But all in all we sure had fun
Up there on that summer range
   And if we don't go back someday soon
Well, something will be mighty strange.

   So, a thanks to you folks up there on the range
For the good time we had this fall
   It sure is nice to have friends like you
And may The Good Lord bless you all.

Plain Tired

{Written while working (?) in a hot
dusty mill for Anaconda Copper}

I'm tired of the roar of the motors
I'm tired of the ore that they dig
    I'm tired of the noise of the cyclones
And the panfeeder that squeals like a pig.

I'm tired of these long steep stairs
That I climb a dozen times a day
    I'm tired of these cut-throat merchants
Who take most all of my pay.

I'm tired of this desolate country
I'm tired of gazing at these barren hills
    I'm tired of drawing my paycheck
And paying it out on bills.

Someday I'll get so tired of it all
I'll terminate and call it a day
    And go back to the horse, the cattle, the mountains
And from there I'll never more stray.

Ah, just to go back to the mountains
Where the streams trickle down from the snow
    Just to be with my horse and the cattle
Of a better life I'll never know.

Just to hear the coyote howling
And the cougar, when he does scream
    An old bear tearing at a hollow log
To me is a heavenly dream.

88

    Just to watch the chipmunks playing
As they scamper to and fro
    Just to watch the eagle soaring
As he scans the earth below.

    Just to gaze at those mountain meadows
With their grass a beautiful green
    Just to look up at the pine trees
Where everything is calm, peaceful and serene.

    Just to watch the deer as they glide along
Down the aisles of the trees
    Just to hear the call of the Mountain Jay
And the humming of the bees.

    Just to drink the water that's pure and cold
That comes from the snow on high
    From up there on the mountain top
Where it seems to meet the sky.

    Just to rise up early in the morning
Feeling so good that I could bust
    It wouldn't be like waking up here
With my lungs full of silica dust.

    And when it starts getting cool in the evenings
A little fire would feel mighty good
    And nothing can smell so nice
As the smoke from yellow pine wood.

When I ride in from my work in the evenings
Feed my horse and put my saddle away
   I feel like a man who has been reincarnated
And has come back as a king for every day.

   And my cabin that sets on the edge of the meadow
In the shade of a big cedar tree
   May not look like much to some people
But it's home sweet home to me.

   And after I've had my fill of beans and meat
Coffee, potatoes and sourdough bread
   I love to sit in my doorway
And listen to the sounds o'er head.

   When the time gets around to nine o'clock
Shown by the clock upon the shelf
   I look at the heavens away up high
And feel at peace with myself.

   It's to this I am returning
Just as soon as I possibly can
   For the lights and noise of the city
Were never meant for this man.

My Little Old Arm Chair

    As I sit here on this old hard bench
Counting loads of copper ore
    It is now I wish my old arm chair
Was here on the upper floor.

    It's just a little old wooden chair
Made out of boards of pine
    An old bolt box and a few old nails
And it fits this body of mine.

    It has a nice reclining back
And a very comfortable seat
    So comfortable it is, in fact
And quite conducive to sleep.

    Each day, when from my arduous tasks
That I have some time to spare
    You will find me in the control room
At rest in my old arm chair.

Me and My Friends

    I'm sitting here in the trailer today
Just lookin' out over the valley
    Just me and my animal friends
Why pardner, that's right up my alley.

    Now, there are wild horses upon the ridges
And cattle in the valley below
    And birds of various kinds and colors
Across the heavens go.

    And old man coyote can be seen
As he slinks up through the sage
    It sure is wonderful to see
All these animals without a cage.

    I never like to see things in cages
Nor tied upon a dog-gone rope
    To have these earthly things a' happening
Takes away all earthly hope.

    That's the way with me and town life
Where you are bounded by houses galore
    And you can't look outside your house
Without looking at someone's window or door.

    Now, I do have a .22 rifle
That I keep beside my bed
    In case some drunk or dope addict
Should try to bash in my poor old head.

But I don't use it on the birds
Nor on the animals passing by
    I may use it on some old tin can
To see if I still have the eye.

But there are a couple of old ravens
That come bothering my feathered friends
    And if my aim is good enough
They'll lose most of their rear ends.

I guess this is the end of this little tale
Of me and my wild life
    Where I don't have much to bother me
Not even my mean old wife.

Growin' Up

When I was a kid a' growin' up
I was raised way up in the mountains
   For me there were no candy stores
Nor any of those ice cream fountains.

   Whenever we would go to town
To look over the human race
   We were given a nickel apiece
And told not to spend it all in one place.

   But those were the days when a nickel
Would take you fast and far
   It was good for a big sack of candy
Or a good old White Owl cigar.

   And if by chance we could happen to get
A two-bit piece all in one sum
   We were as rich as the richest
All rolled up into one.

   But those trips to town were far apart
For not too many had the means
   We'd just stay out there on the homestead
And feast upon venison, sowbelly and beans.

   But we were all pretty happy together
Even though our trips to town weren't frequent
   We all had our work to tend to
And I never knew of a juvenile delinquent.

It was mostly in the spring of the year
When we would have our fun
    Everyone would clean out his barn
After the winter feeding was done.

Then we all would get together
And decorate a barn up bright
    Get a guitar, accordian and fiddle
And dance and dance all night.

Now, some of the women brought cakes and pies
And some brought roasts or a mulligan stew
    While others brought different kinds of food
The men brought jugs of "Mountain Dew."

Oh, we would dance and dance all evening
'Til the sun was shining bright
    Fill up on grub and "Mountain Dew"
And very seldom would there be a fight.

Although everyone there was not related
We were all mighty closeknit
    Should anyone need a helping hand
We were all there to do our bit.

Now, each would help the other
With his hay and grain crop, too
    Mark and brand his calves
And anything else there was to do.

And on X-mas Day we would get together
And of us there was quite a few
    Feast on turkey and all the trimmings
And drink toddies made from that "Mountain Dew."

    The years went by and finally at last
Letters came to that mountain side
    Telling us boys we had been chosen
And had better not try to hide.

    So off we went to World War II
To sight our guns on some Japs
    While some of us were able to return
Others had met with mishaps.

    But nothing was the same as it was before
Before the days of World War II
    When we used to feast and dance together
And partake of that old "Mountain Dew."

    Now, the kids today are quite different
Even those up there in the mountain sage
    Today they want fast cars and gals
And a guaranteed annual wage.

    They no more care for sowbelly and beans
Nor venison made into mulligan stew
    They crave now for champagne and cavier
And like no more that old "Mountain Dew."

Days Gone By

I'm sitting here by the window
At the head of number one (conveyor belt)
   Just sort of reminiscing like
Of places I've seen and things I've done.

   I started out in Modoc
Quite a few years ago
   That's when I was young and nimble
And not so stiff and slow.

   I rode there on a cow ranch
And it was my utter pride
   To jab my bronc in the shoulders
And sit up there and ride.

   Some I rode were quite easy
While others were mighty tough
   After several years of this
I called it deep enough.

   I went to work for a dredging company
In the summer of '38
   But in two years I was back
Swinging on the corral gate.

   I figured I would stay there
Along with my horse and saddle
   But then a letter I received
And I sure had to skedaddle.

It was a letter from Uncle Sam
It seems I was a chosen one
    To go and hunt some Japs
With a great big shootin' gun.

    After two years and six months
Of facing cold and heat
    The army it discharged me
For I had froze my dog-gone feet.

    So back to the ranch I wandered
Thinking it would be the same
    But I sure was fiddle-footed
So I took off again.

    So I traveled around the country
Traveling from here to yon
    And in the fall of '53
I hooked up with Anacon.

    So now I guess I'm a 30-year man
With 25 years to go
    Although my legs are weary
And my step is growing slow.

    But if the time should ever come
When these stairs I can no longer ascend
    I guess I'll go back to the ranch
And in the saddle set my old hind-end.

And if I find that on my horse
I can no longer get astride
   I'll go out behind an old sagebrush
And make that FINAL RIDE.

Trapping Daze

My partner and I set out for the mountains
With traps, grub and tools galore
    We figured when spring came around again
We'd have made a million bucks or more.

We borrowed a cabin from some boys
And promised to take care of it good
    Borrowed a team of old work mares
And hauled in our winter's wood.

We hauled in some yellow pine limbs
And after exhorting some strength
    We took us a new Swede Saw
And cut each limb into length.

We stacked it in an old cabin
That had been there since 1902
    Went out and blazed a trap line
So when it snowed we could follow it through.

Then we sat back and waited for trapping season
I don't remember just when it started
    But before it ever came around
My partner and I had parted.

It seems he had a gal in town
(Who now happens to be his wife)
    And he couldn't bear to be away from her
And live a trapper's life.

So he went back to be with her
Working at some job, I can't remember
    But I stayed on there in the wilds
'Til the latter part of December.

    Well, I set my traps out through the woods
And I tended them morning and night
    But never a thing did I catch
Maybe I didn't have them set just right.

    Now, I was becoming pretty discouraged
With the life of a trapper bold
    And the mercury was hitting down to the bottom
God! but it was getting cold.

    The cabin I had was very nice
But was built for just summer use
    I'd throw in a log and crawl in beside it
For the cold was freezing my juice.

    One night I figured to leave in the morning
After cleaning up camp and buttoning the flap
    But as I went out over the line
Darned if a marten wasn't caught in my trap.

    So after looking that marten over
And figuring how much it would bring when sold
    Things began to look a little better
And the weather didn't seem so cold.

So I stayed there a few days longer
But for the comfort of warmth I did yearn
    Finally it became so durned cold
That the log in the fireplace wouldn't burn.

So I said to myself, "Moffitt, you've had it,"
And the next morning I hit for the logging train
    Went to town and darned near starved
But I never tried trapping again.

But the night before I left the cabin
I was sitting by the fire in a chair
    When the door came flying open
And the outside thermometer stood there.

It said "My dear Mr. Moffitt,
Do I have to get down on my knees
    And beg for some warmth from your fire
As out there I will freeze?"

So I bid it come in by the fire
And absorb some of the little heat
    And early next morning after breakfast
It, my snowshoes and I beat a hasty retreat.

Now, maybe you wonder about the traps
And the tools I left out there
    Well, the following spring I got them
When the weather was a lot more fair.

And the pelt from the only animal I caught
Caught in such despair and disgust
    Well, if the coyotes haven't eaten it
It has long ago turned to dust.

    So that was the end of my trapping
And though I didn't make a dime
    I'd go back and try it again
If I could do it in the summertime.

Clover Valley

I well remember the Clover Valley Ranch
From that summer of '47
    And to anyone who is mountain raised
That is mighty close to heaven.

    I rode there for the Roney brothers
Upon that range so green
    With its stately pines and tamarack
It's as pretty as a person has seen.

    The valley itself is a beautiful sight
With its grass so green in hue
    While the waters of the Susan River
Come wending its passage through.

    The chipmunks play among the limbs
Of those big old tamarack trees
    While the mournful cry of an old coyote
Comes wafting on the breeze.

    The deer come marching from the woods
Stepping so daintily along
    While from the fence top by the cabin
A bird breaks into a beautiful song.

    The horses are eating there in the field
With the grass growing past their knees
    And over there in a hollow log
Is the home of some wild bees.

Oh, the cattle they raise at Clover Valley
Are of the Angus breed
   And you can't show me any that's better
No matter what you might read.

   The beavers work along the stream
Placing trees and mud just so
   Building of their mighty dams
Which mostly adds to the rancher's woe.

   Now, of the animals there were a plenty
That summer I rode in there
   And which vividly brings to my mind
My encounter with a bear.

   I was looking for some cattle one day
And had climbed to a mountain top
   Just riding nonchalantly along
When into view an old bear did pop.

   She was tearing apart a rotten log
To get at those those lucious grubs
   And playing there behind her
Were her two fat playful cubs.

   Well, she looked at me and I looked at her
Then on her hind legs she did stand
   I'll tell you, folks, I wasn't long
In leaving that piece of land.

And as she stood on her hind legs
She looked as big as a house
    And though I figured I was a man
I felt more like a little old mouse.

    I turned my horse back down the mountain
But kept looking back over my shoulder
    And wondered how fast this nag could run
Should that bear become a little more bolder.

    But I guess all she wanted me to do
Was to get the hell out of there
    And folks, that's just what I did do
While muttering a little prayer.

    Maybe you think my sand is lacking
Without much intestinal fortitude
    But folks, don't mess with a mother bear
Out there in the solitude.

Old Nevada
{1988}

I wandered over from California
Just to see what I could see
    And landed here in old Nevada
In this good old land of the free.

    I tried cowboyin' and I tried minin'
(Which took up most of my life)
    And in the midst of my wandering
I found myself a wife.

    When I first came to old Nevada
I wasn't too much sold
    I could have gone right back over the line
To where the streams run clear and cold.

    But I stayed in this good old state
Where they raise cattle and mine for gold
    And the longer I stayed and worked here
My interest sure took hold.

    I found there was much of interest
And not all in a bar or casino
    Nor in the bigger cities of the state
Like Las Vegas or in Reno.

    It's out in the open where I see the charm
Of this high desert, without peer
    And I don't need a church or parson
To let me know that God is near.

    You can stand there on a hill
And in gazing all around
    You can see old Mother Nature
Has had a hand in all things to be found.

    With wild flowers growing there
And the sage like water flowing to the hills
    The multi-colors of the mountains
Will give you many thrills and chills.

    Though the mountains are bare of trees
And the streams are far apart
    There is something about all this
That tugs at the strings of your heart.

    Now I don't mean I've turned my back
On the country of forests and streams
    But to put the two together
Sure makes for some beautiful dreams.

    The natives of Nevada
And many of the other kind
    Are the salt of this great land
And the best that you will find.

    Although I was born and raised in California
I have been here for 40 years or so
    And I reckon I'll continue to live here
'Til my ashes are scattered to the hills and desert below.

Bridgeport Valley and the Circle H Ranch

I went into Bridgeport Valley
In the spring of 1948
    Got a job there on a ranch
That is known as the Circle H.

The ranch sets there in the valley
Where everything is pretty and green
    With wild peach growing there
It's as beautiful as you have seen.

It's where the cattle graze on the meadows
And the deer roam the hills
    The horses in the pastures
Will give you many thrills.

The ranch was started in 1861
By the grandfather of the elder Stan
    At the beginning of the Civil War
In the days when you had to be all man.

He built his ranch out on the flat
Where the "Old Man of the Mountain" could look down
    And see what was going on
At the ranch and on into town.

When I was there on the ranch
Stanley, Sr. was the boss
    Now I'm telling you and it is true
He was really a good old hoss.

Yes, he was a prince of a fellow
As good as you will find
    Though he was serious in nature
He was also very kind.

He knew horses and he knew cattle
And all phases of this stock
    You went to him for good advice
As his was solid as a rock.

And there working beside him
And not shirking at any chore
    Was his very nice wife and helpmate
The indomitable and able Lenore.

It is a combination dude and cow ranch
Where they raise Hereford cattle and Morgan horses
    And when we were working cattle
The dudes came out in forces.

We had darn good times up there
The dudes, cowboys and kitchen staff
    Everyone was full of fun
And always ready for a laugh.

We would ride up into Buckeye Canyon
Looking for horses or for cattle
    With enough dudes in tow
To look like we were going into battle.

Some of them were good riders
While others weren't so good
  Though they got in the road a lot
We all understood.

  We would ride up to Honeymoon Flat
Where we'd have a good old steak fry
  Ate so much steak and all the trimmings
'Til we thought that we might die.

  Then we'd ride to Robinson Creek
Swim and have a lot of fun
  Then meander back to the ranch
Whenever the party was done.

  Yes, we had great times up there
Where the "crags" looked down on us below
  It sure would be nice to relive them
Those times with friends so long ago.

Little Big or Big Enuff

    Big Enuff was a sorrel colt
With four white-stockinged legs
    His actions they were graceful
And he walked like he was stepping on eggs.

    I bought him from a rider
Who came through with a bunch of "bangs"
    I wondered how that nifty colt
Ever got mixed up with that bunch of mustangs.

    When the rider said he'd take $2.50
For any bronc in the bunch
    I got so blamed excited
I almost forgot to eat my lunch.

    Anyway, when he told me that
Over to the bunkhouse I did bolt
    Shook out everything I had for dough
'Cause I sure wanted that sorrel colt.

    I gave the money to that rider
For that colt I had a need
    I sure didn't want him going to Petaluma
To end up as chicken feed.

    For that's where this rider was headin'
With that Nevada mustang bunch
    To be ground up and put in a trough
For some damned old chicken's lunch.

Now, I handled Little Big (as I sometimes called him)
With a lot of tender lovin' care
   And had him following like a dog
When, on the ranch, I went anywhere.

I worked him pretty easy
For he was too young on which to sit
   Just fooled with him, let him carry a kid's saddle
And let him get used to a snaffle bit.

Then I started riding him gently
When he was two or past
   It was then I felt that he
Would be pretty dog-gone fast.

As time went by, I worked him more
Cuttin' cows and ropin' with him
   On calves that weren't too big
'Cause I didn't want him to dim.

At last he became a four-year-old
And I had him trained pretty fair
   He could sneak right up on a calf
And never turn a hair.

We held little jack-pot rodeos
Where you put two-bits in a pot
   Then, it was quite a bit of dough
But today it isn't a lot.

When I roped off of Big Enuff
I figured I had the money won
    If I could throw my loop straight and true
Off that little sorrel son-of-a-gun.

When I had any riding to do
I had that little bronc between my knees
    Because anything you wanted
He was always willing to please.

Then I had to go into the service
So I left Little Big there to roam
    The owner said he would never be used
'Til I was finished and came back home.

And although they didn't use him
There had to come that day
    When he was so badly wire cut*
That he had to be put away.

So I bid you good-bye, Little Big
And I know up there on that range
    We two shall go ropin' and ridin' again
Or I'll think it mighty strange.

* a cougar chased him and some others through some barbed wire fences.

The Big Depression
{Of the 1930's}

    I was brought up during the Big Depression
Some 60 years or so ago
    It was a time of very little money
And people's grub was awfully low.

    Jobs were scarce as hen's teeth
In fact, there was hardly a one
    If you couldn't make it by yourself
Then let me tell you, you were done.

    There wasn't any welfare to speak of
Not as people know it today
    There might be a can of stew from World War I
Or "hard tack" that they gave away.

    But there wasn't any food stamps
WIC or anything like that
    There wasn't anything at all
That would make a person fat.

    I remember the corn, bean and other fields
Where farmers couldn't sell all their crops
    They'd open up the gates to the people
And they'd pick 'til they would drop.

    I remember the steers in the feed lot
That were both fat and sound
    And if they could be sold
They would bring 3 cents a pound.

I remember the big old hogs in the fattening pen
On the yonder side of the fence
    And if they could be sold
They'd bring about 5 cents.

    Those were some of the prices
That the ranchers and farmers got
    If things weren't given away
They would lie in the fields and rot.

    In 1938, things opened up a little
And prices began to raise
    People loosened up a lot
And were singing, "Oh, Happy Days!"

    It was about this time when wages and commodities
Were running even and doing well
    But as years passed by
They sure did go to hell.

    Prices began to soar
While wages stayed in a rut
    It took more and more figuring
To fill a person's gut.

    Now today they are so far apart
A person just doesn't know what to do
    It's getting back to those times
Of 60 years ago that I knew.

    Even today I still clean my plate
As many people do
    It wasn't that I missed any meals
But I sure postponed quite a few.

    Poor? You better believe it
I went to dances dressed in my best
    And won first place
In a hard time contest.

Smith Valley

    Smith Valley is one of the prettiest spots
That ever I did happen to see
    And though I didn't live there long
It always seems like home to me.

    It lies at the base of the Pine Nut Mountains
And on the other side the desert lies
    With the green of the valley floor
And the blue of the big open skies.

    It's where the ranches dot the valley
And the cattle, horses and sheep roam
    Where the farmers plant their crops
In some of the richest loam.

    Where everyone is nice and congenial
And as happy as a clam
    Where everyone knows his neighbor and his faults
But doesn't give a damn.

    There is a big community hall
That sets there in Wellington town
    And when there is anything going on
People do things up brown.

    There is another little town
About four or five miles away
    The name of it is Smith
And it's been there forever and a day.

    Neither town is very big
A fact that I enjoy
    For the big towns and the cities
Were never meant for this old boy.

    I'd like to go back there to live
But I guess now that I never will
    For I am up there in the ancient age
And too far over the hill.

Reminiscing

I motored up to my old stomping grounds
In the northeast country of California state
   In the county of Modoc
That to me still is great.

And as I rode around Big Valley
My mind started wandering back
   To my youthful years of ranch life
And the days I spent in an old line shack.

   At fourteen I went to work as a chore boy
Up there on the old C.W.C.*
   Fed some stock, milked a cow or two
Or whatever there happened to be.

   At sixteen, I graduated to 'cowboy'
And was put out on the Pit River, the south branch
   Out there in a cabin all alone
About 10 miles from the ranch.

   There were about 300 head of steers
That I had to overlook
   And if I didn't want to go hungry
I had to learn how to cook.

   I ate a lot of burned or uncooked grub
Before I got it right
   But before I got the hang of bisquits
I knew I had been in a fight.

Then you had to start from scratch
If you wanted anything to eat
    Nothing came in packages, like today
That all you have to do is heat.

I stayed there for a year or so
And learned to ride a pretty good saddle
    Then I got itchy feet and went
To where they had some wild-eyed cattle.

I had a couple of high ridin' cousins
That didn't have an ounce of fear
    And we cut, ear-marked and branded the calves
Of those cows who could run like deer.

We would bring in unbroke horses
From out of the Indian Mountains
    And some of those old nags
Sure got me to doubtin'.

Doubtin' whether I could ride these broncs
For they sure looked big and rough
    But I sure was going to give it a try
'Cause I was young and tough.

Well, we gentled them up a little
Then we picked out what we would need
    Some we turned back to the mountains
The old and crippled were sold for chicken feed.

Now, I'm going to tell you something
Something that is hard to believe
  But I'm not telling you some 'windy'
And I ain't one to deceive.

  We brought in a bunch of broncs one time
And put them in a corral we had there
  Darned if there wasn't an antelope
That wouldn't leave a black mare.

  I had always heard that an antelope wouldn't jump
But we found out that was a lie
  For when we got after him with our ropes
Over that six-foot fence he did fly.

  He got a running start at that fence
And over the top he did sail
   It wasn't but a few seconds all we could see
Was the white flag of his tail.

  But I guess everything has an ending
Old Uncle Sam saw to that
  For he sent us each a letter of greeting
And told us not to scat.

  So there my reminiscing ended
And no more did I let it roam
   I mounted my four-wheel nag
And came on back to Nevada and home

*{C.W. Clark Company}

The School Fiasco

With the economy shot to hell
And people being laid off every day
With people going homeless and hungry
The school goes on its merry way.

Now, I'm not against education
I think that education is fine
But I think if others have to,
Then schools should hold the line.

Do we need all these high-priced people
That in colleges are so grossly over-paid
Do we need all these school leaders in the counties
Where each aide seems to have their aide?

Now, this isn't meant for the average teachers
Who are in there doing their best
To give the kids a good education
But we can sure get rid of some of the rest.

Can't we cut down on the sports activities
Where kids are bused around the state
To go to different schools
And there in games participate?

I know this is good for their moral
But I would hope for some transformation
Don't put it all on the taxpayers
Let them furnish their own transportation.

I'll probably get some flack from this
But for flack I have a thirst
    I'll not bother with the 5th Amendment
I'll just take the 1st.

Young'uns "Little and Big"

You say it costs a lot to raise a child
Well, on that I'll have to agree
    But if it wasn't for the kids
What kind of a world would this be?

They will wrap you around their little fingers
And lead you to wherever they want to go
    They look up at you with trusting eyes
And you hate like heck to say, "No."

I've heard it said, "Those Terrible Two's"
But I don't think that's so true
    What is worse, as I see it
Is a kid of 12 going on 22.

To get back to raising a child
Sure, it costs a lot of "Jack"
    But what costs more is when they leave home
And then come wandering back.

They'll give you a sad tale of how sick they are
But they know it's a helping hand you'll give
    They may tell you they've come home to die
But you know darn well they've come home to live.

So, I'll take the little folk anytime
With their honest and trusting eyes
    Than to mess with the older ones
Who don't mind telling you some lies.

Dr. Miller, Veterinarian
{At His Retirement Party, March 20, 1992}*

    Why do some people pass themselves off
As something that they ain't?
    Some of the things they say they are
Would make a strong person faint.

    We have just such a person
Who lives here in our valley
    And at telling tall tales
Seems to be right up his alley.

    He tells tales of his healing ways
Among the animals of the west
    Such as horses, cattle, sheep, dogs and cats
He will tell you he is the best.

    But I notice most of the animals die
Upon which he has plied his trade
    No, there's very few of them
That ever make the grade.

    I wonder if animal doctors
Have to take the oath as other doctors do
    If he did, I don't think it did any good
And I believe that this is true.

    You know as well as I do what I wrote above is B.S.
The stuff that makes the grass grow and grow
    'Cause Doc is a darned good vet
And one of the better people I know.

There are those who may disagree
And their remarks may be sharp as a knife
    But hell, why to worry
That's the way of life.

    I guess you know now the man is Doc Miller
A man big and tall
    A man of great distinction
And liked mighty well by all.

    A man when he gives his word
Will see it through to the end
    A man who is honest and trustworthy
And many people call him "Friend."

    He is a vet in our neck of the woods
And as I say, a darned good one is he
    If it wasn't for this man of medicine
Where would our sick and lame animals be?

    He is very kind and gentle
With all the various kinds of stock
    I hardly know what his first name is
As people around here just call him "Doc."

    But I guess now he's a' goin' fishin'
And a skiing down the slope
    I hope he doesn't hang himself
By giving himself too much rope.

Now that I've buttered you up, Doc
And I tried to do it pretty nice
    Maybe you'll treat a sick horse for me
For, let's say, about half the price?

{This is an old saying:}

    As you go into retirement or on through life
No matter what your goal
    Keep your eyes upon the doughnut
And not upon the hole.

    *Dr. Titus asked me -- more like, told me -- to write a poem for Doc Miller's retirement. She said to make the first few verses "giving him hell." Then, "butter him up good." This is the result.

The Senior Center

    We went over to the Senior Center
To a birthday dinner, it was
    I don't know why we went there
Unless it was just becuz.

    Just becuz we wanted to see
If what people said was true
    Of how they loaded up your plate
And it only costs a buck or two.

    Well, it sure was true alright
For the meal was simply grand
    And the people are very friendly
As they offer you their hand.

    The kitchen staff is very nice
They really know their job
    They go at their work in a professional way
They don't go by guess or by God.

    There are those who make swell music
And sing the songs I used to sing
    It isn't that botched up "heavy metal"
These songs are more like the breath of spring.

    Then there is Wanda, my main gal
Who is 'head honcho' over the whole shebang
    She really runs everything right
And looks out for the gang.

The building itself is very nice
With the new addition added to it
    You can play pool, dance, read
Or just plain sit.

    I guess most of us have kids
And them we would like to see
    When they grow out of their childish ways
Enjoy this place as much as we.

    I guess you know we'll be going back
Where they gather around the piano to sing
    Oops, wait just a minute --
Didn't I hear the chow bell ring?

Vote

    I went over on the courthouse lawn
To listen to what the 'wannabe' politicians had to say
    They weren't too bad in looks and talking
But you wonder if they have the guts to go all the way.

    I guess they'd do as well as some we have
And in some we sure need a change
    Not so much in our local government
But some of those in the higher range.

    Like that gal in congress
Who doesn't seem to have a mind
    And votes the way the president says
That person just isn't the right kind.

    We sure have to get rid of Bush
The friend of the 'upper crust'
    I never have cared for him
I don't believe him you can trust.

    He has given so much money away
To the people of foreign lands
    How we can afford to do that
I sure don't understand.

    In his acceptance speech the other night
He said he would make things great
    Where was he the last four years?
Well, he was a dollar short and an hour late.

And that phoney congress that we have
We sure ought to send them on their ways
   All they do is sit there on their duffs
Waiting for Saturday night and pay days.

   Each eligible person should cast a ballot
And though we all don't ride in the same boat
   We should take advantage of our constitutional right
And get out there and VOTE!!

I'm Proud to be an American and Have the Right to Vote

    The primary election is over
Now the general is staring us in the face
    We hope the votes we cast
Will help our persons win the race.

    We'll amble over to the polling place again
Take that little thing in hand
    And poke the holes for the ones we want
And hope they are the best ones of the band.

    But we never know what we have
Until time passes us by
    The ones we voted in might be duds
But we voted, so we have the right to cry.

    It's these people who never vote
That I have no mercy for
    If they start complaining around my place
I'll kick their butts right out the door.

    For it's these people who scream the loudest
When the persons of their choices fail
    To get into their respective offices
Hell, they have no right to wail.

    So, if you want the right to bitch
You will do like this old goat
    And go to your polling place
And thereby cast your vote.

Don't say that your vote doesn't make a difference
'Cause wouldn't it be a sin
   If the vote you didn't cast
Let a good person out and a bad one in?

   This is one of the times I am the proudest
When I cast my vote for my favorite woman or man
   If they aren't voted into office
I'll know I did the best I can.

   I guess I need a soapbox
From which I can expound the words I wrote
   And I sure will get one
If it will help to get people to vote.

The School Teacher's Dilemma

    Someone asked me if I'd like to teach school
I told them, "Thanks, but no thanks"
    When one of those little hellers cussed me
I would probably put on the spanks.

    Then if I put on the spanks
Some parent would knock my teeth loose
    Stomp my pumpkin head
And have me arrested for child abuse.

    For now it's against the law
To make kids mind in any way, shape or form
    If you yell at, spank or shake one of them
That sure will kick off a storm.

    I wonder who made up these laws
Which are screwy, and that's apparent
    Probably by some non-teacher
Who never was a legitimate parent.

    It used to be in days gone by
If you were onery and bad
    You tried to swear everyone to secrecy
And not let it get back to your dad.*

    But today it is a different story
If you try to correct a child
    The school board and some parents
Seem to go off hog-wild.

Now, I don't believe in child abuse
Or anything of that kind
    But a teacher or a parent
Should have more leeway to make them mind.

    If I was back in my child-producing days
I know that I could
    But with 'Big Brother' interference
I don't believe that I would.

    So they can keep their teaching jobs
Because I don't want to hear anyone bitch
    I'll just keep at this easy job
Of digging this dad-gummed ditch.

    This is an old proverb:

"The reason kids no longer mind
As in days of yore
The razor strap no longer hangs
Behind the kitchen door."

*{ask one who knows!}

Turkey Time

    Old Turkey Time is here again
The best holiday of the year
    With the aroma of different good things
That I hold most dear.

    But the one aroma that is the best
{And it sure makes one perky}
    Is that tantalizing smell
Of a freshly baking turkey.

    And all the cakes and pies
That sit cooling on the shelf
    Sure do make my mouth water
I can hardly contain myself.

    We sit around inside the house
If the weather is on the skids
    But if the weather is good
We go outside and play ball with the kids.

    Finally we are called to the table
By one of our famous cooks
    Some kids have to sit in chairs
On top of a couple of books.

    Finally we all get seated at the table
And there we do pause
    To give thanks to the Lord and Tom Turkey
For each had died for a cause.

After dinner we do up the dishes
But leave what is left of the turkey on the table
    So that we can sit there, nibble and talk
As long as we are able.

    At last the guests leave for home
With their bellies full and tight
    The gastric affects of all that good rich food
Put them in an awful plight.

    So I take my hat off to the Pilgrims
Who with the Indians celebrated in their way
    And to Congress, who finally did something
And made Thanksgiving a holiday.

To Whom it May Concern

I've lived my life to the fullest
I've tried to live it good and clean
   Oh, I know I've kicked over the traces at times
But I never tried to be cruel or mean.

   I've played each hand that was dealt me in life
Some of them were mighty rough
   I've drawn to inside straights and bob-tailed flushes
And sometimes I've been known to pull a bluff.

   But I'm not drawing to straights and flushes
Nor am I pulling any bluff
   When I hope someone is listening up There
When I'm about to call my life deep enough.

   Don't let me be dependent on anyone
Not even my kids or wife
   It wouldn't be fair to them or anyone
And spoil their way of life.

   Don't let any cords or tubes be attached to my body
To help me keep on breathing
   I came into this world slick and clean
I want to be that way when I'm leaving.

   If anyone wants any of my organs
They are welcome to all or any part
   But anyone who would want these old things
Can't be very smart.

    Don't make any fuss over my body
When I quit breathing and go
    Just burn my hide and horns to a crisp
And scatter my ashes to the hills and valleys below.

    Don't put my ashes in some container
And leave it sitting there in the room
    'Cause my wife will beat the hell out of me
With her ever-lovin' broom.

    I guess that about covers my wishes for when I die
As I say, take my ashes away up high
    And let them drift down from the sky
Good-bye, good-bye, good-bye ...

Dr. Robin Titus
{Medicine Woman}

    She went before the county commissioners
And asked them what they could do
    About paying her way through medical school
So that she could be a doctor tried and true.

    They came to a decision and an agreement
That would help her attain her goals
    If she would come back to the country awhile
And doctor some of our poor souls.

    Well, she sure fulfilled her contract
And we were paid back over and above
    For the money spent on her education
To attain the position that she loves.

    She doctored in Yerington for several years
No matter the color, creed or race
    Now she has taken her practice to Smith Valley
This very beautiful place.

    Yes, she has a smaller practice in Wellington
And a nice ranch on Gage Road
    She has never said, but I'll bet a dollar or two
It was a relief to get rid of some of that load.

    She is a very good doctor
As good as you will find
    And as a woman she is tops
So generous and so kind.

    She is well-liked by most everyone
And in the community she is a pillar
    But you have to expect this of her
She's the grand-daughter of my good friend, Alex Miller.

    Now, as I come to the end of this heartfelt poem
To the truthfulness of it I can boast
    I'd like to offer to her
This very sincere toast:

    Here's to my friend and doctor, Robin Titus
    Who never ceases to amaze me
    May she continue her kind and healing ways
    Among the sick, the lame and the lazy.

My Rustler Jeans

    Some people wear Levi Strauss
And I'll tell you, they are fine
    While other people wear Wranglers
Or some other well-known line.

    But I wear Rustler Jeans
That I think are mighty nice
    They fit me just as well
And they cost about half the price.

    They will wear and wear and wear
You can wear them for work or for town
    But after several washings
The zipper keeps sliding down.

    But that doesn't bother me much
'Cause I can take care of that zip
    By making a hook to hold it up
Out of a big old paper clip.

    Some folks may not like the looks of it
{But then, what to them do I owe?}
    It keeps me from being arrested
And covers what I have below.

    Perhaps it isn't the zipper's fault
For I have what you might call a fat gut
    And there to balance it out
Is a big old fat butt.

So, you see, a zipper doesn't have much chance
To do the job it is supposed to do
   It might not be a bad idea
If I was to lose a pound or two.

   So, let people wear what they wish
Don't stop them by any means
   But I'll just try to get along
With my good old Rustler Jeans.

Alex Miller
{A Good Friend}

In Smith Valley there lived a man
A man so kind and true
   If you did right by him
He would sure do right by you.

   He came from Russia as a youth
At what age I do not know
   But if Russia knew the good man he'd become
They wouldn't have let him go.

   He would greet each day with a smile
And it would be there the whole day through
   He always had a kind word
For everyone he knew.

   He was as honest as the day is long
And of that people were very fond
   You needed no lawyer person with him
As his word was as good -- or better -- than a bond.

   I lived on a ranch to the south of him
And many times up the irrigation ditch he would walk
   We would meet on the ditch bank
And have a little talk.

   We would talk about the crops and weather
Just about everything in creation
   We saved a lot of people from their faults
And we also saved our wonderful nation.

But now that you have left us, Alex
And have moved on to other parts
    You just can't get rid of us so easily
As you will always be in our hearts.

    Now, when it's our time to go to the "Big Pasture"
To push open the "Pearly Gate"
    Alex will be there to greet us
With that big old smile so great.

    Alex, if you should see St. Peter
Tell him that we would have him to thank
    If he could make a little room for us to talk
Up There on some old ditch bank.

    Now, I'll not say good-bye, Alex
As it is a sad and final adieu
    So, I'll just say so-long, old friend
And I hope to be seeing you.

    A friend (?) read this poem
And had the gall to say,
    "You'll not see Alex, as he is in Heaven
And you are headed the other way."

Some friend.

The Church Stood Up

    In the Methodist Church in Smith Valley
A memorial was held one day
    For a darned good man and citizen
Who had recently passed away.

    His name was Alex Miller
He was a farmer of the land
    If someone was in honest trouble
Alex would be there to lend a helping hand.

    When I told a fellow I was going
He said, "Oh my God, Boyd -- No!
    The walls will come tumbling down
Like the Walls of Jericho."

    He said that the church would fall right down
For the shock of me in it would be too great
    And that if I had any consideration at all
I would stop out by the gate.

    Well, I half-way believed him
As I crept up to the door
    I wondered if it would come crashing down
And spill upon the floor.

    I kept listening for any strange noise
To come from that Holy House
    To warn me that it was falling in
Smashing me, the others, and the poor church mouse.

But I heard not a sound of stress
No moans, groans and no kind of squeal
    That it would ever fall
As into it I did steal.

But it stood upright, solid
As I sidled into a pew
    I felt so relieved about it
That all I could say was, "Phew!"

Now, I'm going to get even with that man
I'm sure going to make him beg
    'Cause I know now he wasn't telling the truth
And was just pulling my leg.

Our Mothers

There are holidays and then there are holidays
But the one I like as none of the others
   Is the one we celebrate in May
To honor our dear Mothers.

   For Mothers are the kind of people
That we all should love to know
   For they look upon their children
With their hearts all aglow.

   It matters not their children's trouble
Nor the kind of trouble they are in
   The Mother will stand beside them
And help them through -- through thick and thin.

   Then as they grow to adulthood
And go out in the world to see what they can see
   There isn't a Mother who is a Mother
Who wishes they were little, playing around her knees.

   Mothers are a big necessity
As anyone can plainly see
   If it wasn't for our Mothers
Where the heck would we be?

Our Hospital

Our hospital here in Yerington
Isn't too big in size
　But the tender lovin' care they give
Sure would win a blue ribbon prize.

　The doctors and the RN's are professionals
And the LPN's are very much needed, too
　The office force and maintenance workers
All know what to do.

　The Adult Volunteers are very helpful
Especially in the Doctor Mary Wing
　Helping with their bingo games and art crafts
And any other help they can bring.

　The Auxiliary Unit is very important
They help with blood drives and health fairs
　Put on fund raisers and fashion shows
To raise money for the hospital, they'll be there.

　As I say, they are very important
They all do their work with a will
　That's what keeps our hospital perking
And keeps it up on top of the hill.

Mason Valley and Yerington

We took a ride the other day
And came back by way of Weed Heights
   In coming down the newly-made road
We saw some wonderful sights.

   The valley itself is still green in color
And the trees with their leaves of gold
   And the ranches dotting the landscape
Was a view you seldom behold.

   There are several things raised in the valley
But onions and garlic seem to hold sway
   But there are cattle, horses and sheep
And that high-protein alfalfa hay.

   I guess I never did really look at the valley
{But then, I've only been here forty years or so}
   From what I saw on our ride that day
I'll be more aware as around the valley I go.

   The town of Yerington, the only one in the valley
Is not too big, as yet, in size
   But the way businesses and people are moving in
Soon we'll awaken to a big surprise.

   The people in Yerington and the valley
Are as nice as they can be
   They will help in any way they can
And that means a lot to me.

    I hope not to have a Vegas or Reno
Nor a Carson City or even a Gardnerville
    If it should grow that big
I'll head over the eastern hills.

    Maybe over to Reese River Valley
Where there aren't many abodes
    Where there won't be much to bother me
Except rattlesnakes or horny toads.

I bank at the First Interstate Bank
Here in the town of Yerington
    It's here you can wait in line for hours
And eventually get your business done.

    The tellers all are very rude
As they stand behind their stanchions
    They stand there gazing at the ceiling
And dream of living in mansions.

    If they didn't want to wait on you
They reach up and close the stanchion door
    And act like they don't see you
Oh, they treat you mighty poor.

    Now, the three men working there
Aren't too bad in their own way
    But they give you an awful look and frown
If you and your visit overstay.

    I wonder if this is the way they are
As they bask there in their glory
    Or maybe they are afraid
That I'm cutting in on their territory.

    It's supposed to be a full-service bank
But on this I must disagree
    Or else those rooms in the back
Weren't meant for the likes of me.

Now, you know the above is B.S.
That stuff that makes the grass grow green
    For these gals are the best
That you have ever seen.

    They will help you in any way
For they are mighty helpful gals
    And to me and some others
They are a good bunch of pals.

    Yes, they will help you in any way they can
Be it making copies or balancing books
    But what always pleases me most
Is their always pleasant looks.

    Now, the rooms back in the back
Those rooms about which I writed
    I wouldn't think of going back there
Unless, of course, I was invited.

    If I couldn't shoot the bull with the gals
I would feel toward the bank pretty hard
    And get me some old coffee can
And plant my dough in my back yard.

    So I guess I better end this saga
Of me and my banking harem
    'Cause if I make this too sweet and juicy
It sure as hell will scare 'em.

Jaywalking

    On Main Street an elderly man was struck
By a car that was passing by
    I know he wasn't in a cross-walk
But I have often wondered why.

    Why they don't legally make Main Street
One continuous cross-walk, well, I'll say
    From the Golden Rule to City Hall
It's that way, anyway.

    I know and there's others who know
That a lot of cars don't go very slow
    On Main Street or any other street
They romp down on the gas and go.

    Besides, the cross-walks are too far apart
For a lot of us whose legs aren't so spry and strong
    We can walk just so far
Then we get a catch in our "get alongs."

    And the way Yerington is growing
Today it isn't so small
    We can't always park where we wish
In fact, it's getting hard to park at all.

    So make Main a continuous cross-walk
As from crossing to crossing is quite a hike
    It's too darned far for me
That's one reason I ride my bike.

    Or jaywalk.

For All Young People Everywhere

    I've been to high school rodeos
I'll tell you, they are grand
    I would have liked them better had I been on a horse
Instead of up there in the grand-stand.

    The kids all did real well
At roping, riding and such
    I really enjoyed the barrel racing
Which I like very much.

    The girls, on their horses, race around the arena
Carrying the colors so happy and proud
    And get a thunderous ovation
From everyone in the crowd.

    I'd much rather watch these young people
As they participate in their shows
    Than to watch the professionals
In their big-time rodeos.

    Now, this is not meant for just rodeo kids
It's meant for all who participate in sports
    You can look at them and know
That most all will be the right sort.

    For any who participate in sports
And give it all they've got
    Won't be joining any gangs
Nor be out there smoking pot.

So, my hat's off to all these young adults
Who are doing the best they can
   To grow into adulthood
And to be a better woman or man.

   Yes, it's nice to see them participate
And hope in the future they will be
   The ones to lead our great nation
And keep it safe and free.

The People and the Valley of Bridgeport

    I traveled down from the north country*
Down Highway 395
    Didn't have much in mind
Just enough to keep me alive.

    I had a dollar or two in my pocket
And a car that ran fairly well
    Just traveling nonchalantly along
When I viewed a sight that over me cast a spell.

    'Twas the sight of Bridgeport Valley
Which was so green in hue
    And the waters of the East Walker
Came wending their passage through.

    I thought to myself, 'This is it'
Just like Brigham Young with his band
    I figured I could never do better
And a job I was able to land.

    I worked for the Hunewill Circle H
A combination dude and cow outfit
    Doing everything from wranglin' dudes to cowboyin'
Just anything to make me and the ranch show a profit.

    I met a lot of nice people on the ranch
And also in town
    They are the kind after a handshake
Will never let you down.

Yes, it's mighty nice country up there
But like most places the people are mostly new
    I imagine though that most of them
Are as nice as the ones I knew.

    Most of the old-timers have passed away
Of those left, I don't think I'd know over three or four
    The Bettencourts, Dan Bryant, his mother & Ken Miller
I doubt if there is anymore.

    I like to go back pretty often
Especially on the Fourth of July
    To watch the parade and other festivities
All are mighty good and that's no lie.

    So, my hat is off to everything up there
For it's all right up my alley
    Long live the people up there
And that beautiful Bridgeport Valley.

*Susanville, California, May 1948

Bill and Rose Kramer, Wonderful People

    In Modoc County, California, there lived a man
And a darned good man was he
    He had a ranch along the Pit River
As a youth he came from Germany.

    He worked at anything he could get
And accumulated much property and land
    He hired me on when I was a boy
And molded me into a pretty fair hand.

    Although my name is Boyd, he called me "Boyt"
Due to his German accent
    But I didn't mind because I found
It caused no harm, it caused no accident.

    When we were haying, he paid me 25 cents a day extra
To help him milk a few old cows
    Of course, there was the separating of milk to do
And the slopping of those big old sows.

    In those days, 25 cents was pretty good money
In fact, it was darn good pay
    For in the 1930's
Pay was a dollar a day.*

    He was a stickler for a person to be on time
And he had the time right down to the letter
    Often, when I was a few minutes late
I would hear him say, "Boyt, you've got to do better!!"

As I say, he molded me into a pretty fair hand
And now I am glad to relate
   That but for an emergency
On a job, I was very seldom late.

   We started at four in the morning
And we'd find ourselves in a fix
   If we weren't through with the chores on time
For breakfast was straight up and down at six.

   Now, his wife, Rose, was also a stickler for time
As everyone had other work to do
   So you better be on time
If you wanted any food to chew.

   And if you left anything on your plate
She sure didn't believe in waste
   You would have it there the next meal
And you better give it a pretty fair taste.

   But she was a very considerate lady
It didn't matter if you were tight or loose
   Here came Rose to help you
With her Castor Oil and Orange Juice.

   No matter which was bothering you
I am right here to say
   Though it was mighty vile medicine
The darned stuff worked either way.

Now, when I die and maybe go to Heaven
And stop at the "Pearly Gate"
    Rose will be there with Orange Juice & Castor Oil
And Bill will say, "Boyt! Why are you so late?!!"

    Yes, I learned a lot from these people
I learned to clean up my plate
    I learned not to let Rose know how I felt
And from Bill I learned not to be late.

*A dollar a day, plus room & board.

The Horse Shoein' Man
{Dedicated to Gary Nelson, a Friend of Mine}

    Now, a horse shoein' man need not be a big man
But he must be mighty strong
    So he can handle any of the hay burners
Should they happen to go wrong.

    He carries with him his shoeing tools
An anvil and a forge run by propane
    A first-aid kit and some medicine
Should he come into any pain.

    There is a chance he might get hurt
By anyone of the band
    Such as a cut across his legs
Or a gouge taken out of a hand.

    He drives up to where he's going to shoe
Climbs out and hitches up his pants
    Ambles over to the fence
And proceeds to drown some ants.

    He stops and puts on a leather apron
Or maybe an old pair of chaps
    To protect himself from nail cuts
Or any other mishaps.

    Then he will catch up an old bronc
And tie him up short
    Then maybe the shoer will pass some gas
And the bronc will let out a big snort.

It's a back-breaking job and that's for sure
As between or over his legs he places a hoof
   So that he can see what he's doing
And hope that he don't goof.

   Just about the time he has a nail or two
Hammered half-way through a shoe
   The old hammer head will make a lunge
But for his leathers, his legs would be dug into.

   But then there is the gentle stock
That don't mind being shod at all
   If the shoer doesn't hold them up
They will go to sleep and fall.

   Or maybe there will be a playful nag
{And if the shoer's butt is turned just right}
   Will stretch its neck around
And take one hell of a bite.

   Each spring on the old Circle H
There were about 60 head to shoe and keep shod
   If I never shoe another horse
That will be too soon, so help me God!

   Now, I'll leave the shoeing to you, Gary
For I know this job you will not shirk
   You must be a glutton for punishment
'Cause it's a hell of a lot of work.

I hope not to shoe anymore horses
I'll leave it to those who can
   I guess you can tell by my writings
That I am NOT a horse shoein' man.

The Diamond B Brand
and Old Joe Biglow

    Up in the Madeline Plains country
I rode for the Diamond B Brand*
    And to ride for that outfit
You had to be a damned good hand.

    This was in Lassen County, California
Several long years ago
    The owner was a cantankerous old cuss
By the name of Joe Biglow.

    Yes, he was cantankerous as hell
But I'll give him his due
    He knew one end of a cow from the other
And he sure expected it of you.

    It was on the west side of the Plains
Where we had our summer cow camp
    And nearly every horse I rode there
Tied my belly up into cramps.

    For they had Old Joe's disposition
They were sure a salty bunch
    And many times I lost it
Or couldn't eat my lunch.

    I often heard it said up there
And I don't doubt but what it's so
    That he bought the cast-offs
From out of the rodeos.

Some of them gentled up a little
While the others did not
　　But it seems I got my share
Of the damned bad lot.

　　The real tough ones we sent to some brothers
Who had ranches on the east side of the Plains
　　If they couldn't ride them they tied cowhides
　　　　　　　　　　　　to their tails
Turned them loose and never saw them again.**

　　Some were seen again, alright
Out toward Gerlach on some lonely trail
　　They had run themselves to death
With some of the hides still tied to their tails.

　　But he sure had good fat cattle
That were of the Hereford and Angus strains
　　'Cause the graze was plenty good
Up there on the Madeline Plains.

　　He furnished a good cook and darned good grub
And the place we bunked in wasn't bad
　　But his damned old cantankerousness
Made us all pretty damned mad.

　　But I'll say another thing for Old Joe
He could ride the whole day through
　　And he never asked from any man
What he wasn't able to do.

There is an antelope reserve up there
And we would count them by the score
  I ate so much antelope meat
That I sure as hell didn't want anymore.

  We mixed it up with venison
That we shot up in yonder hills
  For old Joe hated to kill a beef
He claimed they helped pay the bills.

  I rode there for a spell
Then my feet began to itch
  It felt good to get away from that rough stock
And that cantankerous old son-of-a-sich and sich.

*   About 1937

** I didn't like this idea

Hammonton
{Near Marysville, California}

Not far from the Yuba River
Stood a town so quaint and fair
　Where in the spring everything was green
And the scent of flowers filled the air.

Everyone was friendly and congenial
And just as happy as could be
　Each knew each other and their faults
In fact, it was just like one big family.

It was owned by the Yuba Consolidated Goldfields
This little town so fair
　And out to the north and west of it
The land the big old dredgers did tear.

They brought up the earth in their buckets
And each weighed nearly two tons
　They left big rock piles and devastation
Wherever and whenever their work was done.

Yes, they brought up the earth in their buckets
And from this they sorted out the gold
　Sent it to the mint in San Francisco
And there the yellow flakes were sold.

It wasn't nice to see this happening
All the devastation to this earth
　But perhaps it wouldn't have bothered so much
Had it not been the land of one's birth.

At last it came to the townsite
To be dredged for that glittering gold
And for a dollar a piece and the moving
All houses in Hammonton were sold.

So they dredged the site of Hammonton
Left not a single trace of the town
Dug up the earth and left there
No wonder people felt so down.

There were many who worked there a long while
From the time the town was started
And many others would have stayed
But by the Big Depression were parted.

Now, the company there was very good
As many a person will say
The hours weren't long, nor the work too hard
And they were mighty good in their pay.

The company houses were very nice
And they didn't hold you up for rent
The grass and flowers were beautiful
In fact, it was money very well spent.

Then we, as kids, found things to do
{And, at most, we didn't misbehave}
We would swim in those deep dredger ponds
Or go exploring in "Black Bart's Cave."

I can't remember all the people's names
Who lived and worked in Hammonton
    But perhaps I can remember a few
Before my narrative is done.

    There were my uncle and aunt, the Bill Taylors
And the Moffitts, of which I am one
    The Hasletts, the Hargraves, the Scotts
Then there was old Lew Oakes and his son.

    There were the Brophys, Campers and Lambrechts
Harry and Gus Weldon and their families, too
    The McFarlanes, the Colemans, the Raetzes
Whose members numbered quite a few.

    Bess, Holmes, McGovern, Bird and Dooley
Ewart, Darst, Nutely, Thatcher and Payne
    Himes, Houseman, Campbell and Jory
Lepage, Gray, White, Sylva and Dewayne.

    There were the Sinnots, the Wehunts, the Glenns
Workman, Clark, Aaronson, Stroup and the Doles
    Goss, Monohan, Criddle and McCarthy
Then there were many more dear souls.

    I wish I could think of more of the names
Of those folks who were from Hammonton town
    So, forgive me for slighting the others
And for not putting their names down.

Now, although the town is gone
With the work and devastation done
   There shall always be a warm place in my heart
For the people and place of Hammonton.

Clara and Lowell Hillygus

The old Texaco station will be lonely
After the passing of one of the best women, far or near
    She sold gasoline and washed windshields
There on that corner for nearly 55 years.

    When she came out with a towel and wet sponge
To knock off some dirt
    You didn't like to tell her not to
As she always looked sad and hurt.

    She was really a good kind-hearted person
Who never failed to lend a helping hand
    To the down and out people in need
She was about the best in the land.

    Her husband, Lowell, died in 1978
Due to cancer, that dreaded disease
    A disease that's so ravaging
It will bring strong people to their knees.

    So, now she has gone to be beside him
A place where she has wanted to be
    God Bless you, Clara and Lowell
You both were mighty good to me.

    Yes, you both were mighty fine people
And regardless of what some others may say
    I know I'll be going to Heaven
And I'll see you up There some day.

p.s.

    Clara, you might have to learn a new job
If so, I know you will handle it with care
    It will have to be other than a service station
As I don't think there are gas and windshields up There.

The Keyless Man

    This talk about a key man
Sure does make me sore
    For the only key I know of
Is to lock and unlock a door.

    I guess there are different kinds of keys
And each one has its place
    But a key man on any job
Just isn't in the human race.

    There are people who are mighty important
To any job that is done
    But it takes each and everyone of us
To get the battle won.

    From the laborers and the spotters
And everyone enroute
    Everyone plays a part
To get the copper to Butte.

    Now, if our jobs were not important
In handling this copper ore
    Just stop for a moment and wonder
What has the company hired you for?

    So, talk to me not of a key man
As it causes me such sorrow
    For if anyone of us died tonight
The work would still go on tomorrow.